THE COMPLETE GUIDE TO

Working *with* Worms

Using the Gardener's Best Friend for Organic Gardening and Composting

by WENDY VINCENT

The Complete Guide to Working with Worms: Using the Gardener's Best Friend for Organic Gardening and Composting

Library of Congress Cataloging-in-Publication Data

Vincent, Wendy M., 1975-
  The complete guide to working with worms : using the gardener's best friend for organic gardening and composting / by Wendy Vincent.
     p. cm.
  Includes bibliographical references and index.
  ISBN 978-1-60138-599-4 (alk. paper) -- ISBN 1-60138-599-4 (alk. paper) 1. Earthworm culture. 2. Vermicomposting. 3. Compost. 4. Organic gardening. I. Title.
  SF597.E3V56 2012
  639'.75--dc23
                                        2011049584

Printed in the United States

PHOTOGRAPHS AT DIRTY WORMS: Lynzee Marmor
ILLUSTRATIONS: Phil Hawn

PROJECT MANAGER: Gretchen Pressley
BOOK PRODUCTION DESIGN: T.L. Price • design@tlpricefreelance.com
PROOFREADING: C&P Marse • bluemoon6749@bellsouth.net
FRONT COVER DESIGN: Meg Buchner • megadesn@mchsi.com
BACK COVER DESIGN: Jackie Miller • millerjackiej@gmail.com

Printed on Recycled Paper

A few years back we lost our beloved pet dog Bear, who was not only our best and dearest friend but also the "Vice President of Sunshine" here at Atlantic Publishing. He did not receive a salary but worked tirelessly 24 hours a day to please his parents.

Bear was a rescue dog who turned around and showered myself, my wife, Sherri, his grandparents Jean, Bob, and Nancy, and every person and animal he met (well, maybe not rabbits) with friendship and love. He made a lot of people smile every day.

We wanted you to know a portion of the profits of this book will be donated in Bear's memory to local animal shelters, parks, conservation organizations, and other individuals and nonprofit organizations in need of assistance.

– Douglas & Sherri Brown

PS: We have since adopted two more rescue dogs: first Scout, and the following year, Ginger. They were both mixed golden retrievers who needed a home.

Want to help animals and the world? Here are a dozen easy suggestions you and your family can implement today:

- *Adopt and rescue a pet from a local shelter.*
- *Support local and no-kill animal shelters.*
- *Plant a tree to honor someone you love.*
- *Be a developer — put up some birdhouses.*
- *Buy live, potted Christmas trees and replant them.*
- *Make sure you spend time with your animals each day.*
- *Save natural resources by recycling and buying recycled products.*
- *Drink tap water, or filter your own water at home.*
- *Whenever possible, limit your use of or do not use pesticides.*
- *If you eat seafood, make sustainable choices.*
- *Support your local farmers market.*
- *Get outside. Visit a park, volunteer, walk your dog, or ride your bike.*

Five years ago, Atlantic Publishing signed the Green Press Initiative. These guidelines promote environmentally friendly practices, such as using recycled stock and vegetable-based inks, avoiding waste, choosing energy-efficient resources, and promoting a no-pulping policy. We now use 100-percent recycled stock on all our books. The results: in one year, switching to post-consumer recycled stock saved 24 mature trees, 5,000 gallons of water, the equivalent of the total energy used for one home in a year, and the equivalent of the greenhouse gases from one car driven for a year.

Author Dedication and Acknowledgments

This book is dedicated to my mother, who had the unfortunate task of sticking her hands in my childhood pockets to remove worms and other assorted bugs before doing the laundry.

I would also like to thank my husband and our children for their gift to me of the many Saturdays I spent alone at the local library to work on this book. Thank you for your enduring love, encouragement, and unequivocal support. I would also like to extend a special thank you to our daughter, who helps maintain our basement worm bin with great love and care.

Table of Contents

Chapter 2: The Gardener's Best Friend — Worms 49

Chapter 3: Getting Started — Setting up the Worm Composting Bin..61

Chapter 5: Caring for Your Worm Bin.. 107

Chapter 6: Common Concerns in the Worm Bin 125

Chapter 9: Using Worm Compost and Castings.................... 165

Chapter 10: Growing Worms and Vermicompost for Sale 175

Chapter 11: Marketing your Worm Business Via the Internet 227

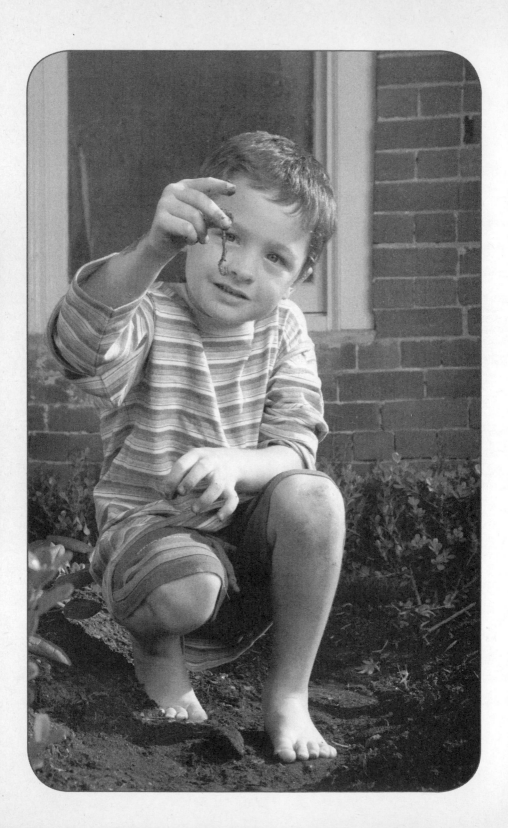

Song of the Worm
by Eliza Cook

THE worm, the rich worm, has a noble domain
In the field that is stored with its millions of slain;
The charnel-grounds widen, to me they belong,
With the vaults of the sepulchre, sculptured and strong.
The tower of ages in fragments is laid,
Moss grows on the stones, and I lurk in its shade;
And the hand of the giant and heart of the brave
Must turn weak and submit to the worm and the grave.

Daughters of earth, if I happen to meet
Your bloom-plucking fingers and sod-treading feet—
Oh! turn not away with the shriek of disgust
From the thing you must mate with in darkness and dust.
Your eyes may be flashing in pleasure and pride,
'Neath the crown of a Queen or the wreath of a bride;
Your lips may be fresh and your cheeks may be fair—
Let a few years pass over, and I shall be there.

Cities of splendour, where palace and gate,
Where the marble of strength and the purple of state;
Where the mart and arena, the olive and vine,
Once flourished in glory; oh ! are ye not mine?
Go look for famed Carthage, and I shall be found

In the desolate ruin and weed-covered mound;

And the slime of my trailing discovers my home,

'Mid the pillars of Tyre and the temples of Rome.

I am sacredly sheltered and daintily fed

Where the velvet bedecks, and the white lawn is spread;

I may feast undisturbed, I may dwell and carouse

On the sweetest of lips and the smoothest of brows.

The voice of the sexton, the chink of the spade,

Sound merrily under the willow's dank shade.

They are carnival notes, and I travel with glee

To learn what the churchyard has given to me.

Oh! the worm, the rich worm, has a noble domain,

For where monarchs are voiceless I revel and reign;

I delve at my ease and regale where I may;

None dispute with the worm in his will or his way.

The high and the bright for my feasting must fall—

Youth, Beauty, and Manhood, I prey on ye all:

The Prince and the peasant, the despot and slave;

All, all must bow down to the worm and the grave.

Reducing, Recycling, and Red Worms

"All the fertile areas of this planet have at least once passed through the bodies of earthworms."

CHARLES DARWIN

As a child, I loved to play in the dirt. I still do. There is nothing like running your hands through a rich, dark soil and feeling the earth as it slides between your fingers, especially dirt that has been warmed by the sun. And the smell; nothing quite compares to that earthy, musty smell of good soil. Any gardener will tell you that.

Not to mention, the dirt is where my friend the worm makes his home, along with a bunch of other little neighboring creatures. I always was fascinated by these little wriggling things and, much to my mother's dismay, would often free them from their earthly homes and carry them around in my pockets. What worm would not want to go on an adventure in a little girl's pocket? Looking back, I am not sure whom I feel more sorry for, the worms that met their untimely deaths in my pockets, or my mother, who had the task of emptying my pockets out before doing the wash.

 Growing up, we always had a vegetable garden in our backyard that was resplendent with a good worm supply. Back then, I did not realize the reason our dirt was so rich and dark was that my worm friends worked so hard under the soil to make it that way. Today, I have worms living in my garden beds and in my basement. Those in my garden beds are working hard to make my soil the dark, nutrient-rich medium that grows my perennials, vegetables, and herbs. The ones in my basement eat our household garbage and make a wonderful fertilizer for the garden beds and potted plants.

Worms, through their natural process of eating waste and turning it into a nutrient-filled by-product, are an ideal way to reduce waste, recycle, and create a wonderful compost for your plants. Through this book, I hope to introduce you to my friend, the invaluable earthworm, and guide you through the process of recycling through composting with worms. I also will give some suggestions on fun and educational activities to get the whole family involved in the process. The activities are designed to be simple, use items you may already have on hand, and be informative and educational. You might want to invest in a single three-ring binder or a notebook throughout the process to keep track of the activities, questions, and what you have learned. Kids also may want to make their own drawings to include in the binder as well.

Benefits of Recycling Through Vermicomposting

Composting, by definition, is a natural process by which organic waste is biologically reduced into **humus**, a dark blackish-brown material of partially or fully decayed organic matter. The process begins when a plant or animal dies and is attacked by **microorganisms**, tiny organisms that cannot be seen, present in the soil. The resulting humus becomes a nutrient-rich natural fertilizer for plants. Rain, heat, fallen leaves, animal waste, dying plants, and other organic elements all can play a part in the natural cycle of composting. When the parts combine in just the right way, **fungi** (organisms that reproduce by spores) begin to grow, and microorganisms help facilitate the process of breaking the materials down. The resulting product is Mother Nature's way of naturally recycling these materials into a viable fertilizer used to establish and promote healthy growth. In nature, worms promote this process and play a vital role in the composting cycle.

Re-creating this natural process is also called composting. Gardeners have been using this process for thousands of years to amend their soil and create healthier and more productive yields. Today, composting is an integral part of the production of food and plants. Home gardeners, landscapers, and professional growers all benefit from various methods of composting to create healthier and larger crops. Composting also is considered a natural and beneficial way in which to reuse and recycle waste. Vermicomposting, as a key consideration, is one of the simplest forms of composting that helps reduce household waste.

In addition to adding nutrients back into the earth, composting, and vermicomposting in particular, also offers a host of other benefits that come from recycling organic matter. The Environmental Protection Agency (EPA) noted that in 2005, Americans recycled 32 percent of their waste, the equivalent of nearly 79 million tons. In addition, 62 percent of yard waste is composted. According to their website, the EPA (**www.epa.gov**) estimates that if 100 percent of our food scraps were composted in conjunction with our current recycling practices, we might be able to prevent the equivalent of 20 million metric tons of carbon dioxide emissions each year. That amount is equal to about 3.8 million vehicles' greenhouse gas emissions. And vermicomposting is the ideal method to use in composting food scraps.

The creation and use of compost can result in a variety of environmental benefits. In addition to enriching and revitalizing nutrient-weak soil, compost suppresses plant disease and pests, thereby reducing and eliminating the need for harmful chemical fertilizers. Chemical-laden fertilizers have been shown in studies to have adverse affects on our environment and health, but practicing organic forms of gardening and lawn maintenance without the use of chemicals can help the environment and cut down on the instances of chemical-induced diseases and even global warming.

According to a study done by Stanford University graduate student, Sasha B. Kramer, and published in the Proceedings of the National Academy of Sciences (PNAS, 2006), Kramer found that "fertilizing apple trees with synthetic chemicals produced more adverse environmental effects than feeding them with organic materials."

"The intensification of agricultural production over the past 60 years and the subsequent increase in global nitrogen inputs have resulted in substantial nitrogen pollution and ecological damage," Kramer and her colleagues write. "The primary source of nitrogen pollution comes from nitrogen-based agricultural fertilizers, whose use is forecasted to double or almost triple by 2050."

The study also found that nitrogen compounds from synthetic fertilizer can enter the atmosphere and contribute to global warming. These compounds can also contaminate water. The study shows that the use of "organic fertilizers can play a role in reducing these adverse effects."

The process of vermicomposting also has been shown to facilitate the cleanup of contaminated soils. Composting absorbs odors and can treat semi- and **volatile organic compounds** (VOCs) such as heating fuels, explosives, and **polyaromatic hydrocarbons** (PAHs), all of which can be detrimental to the environment and our well-being. In addition, the vermicomposting process degrades and removes pesticides and wood preservatives. Vermicomposting even is used as a way to dispose of urban waste. As an example, it was reported that during the Sydney Olympic Games in 2000, about 400 million earthworms were used as a form of composting to dispose of the waste and garbage created from the games.

What Does *That* Mean?

Volatile organic compounds, or VOCs, are defined in a variety of ways. Generally speaking, a VOC can either be a man-made or naturally occurring chemical compound that evaporates into the air at a low temperature. VOCs contribute to air pollution but are not considered to be acutely toxic due to their low concentration level. VOCs can, however, affect both the environment and human health. Due to their low level of concentration, symptoms caused by exposure to VOCs are slow to develop and are compounded over time.

Polyaromatic hydrocarbons, or PAHs, also are known as polycyclic aromatic hydrocarbons. PAHs are environmental pollutants and can be found in coal, oil, and tar. PAHs are a by-product produced when these items are burned as fuel. As a pollutant, some of the compounds released have been identified as harmful carcinogens and other cell-damaging components.

All forms of compost, including vermicomposting, can be used to prevent erosion on embankments near bodies of water and deter turf loss from playing fields, roadsides, and golf courses. In addition to being used as an erosion and turf-loss deterrent, all forms of compost also can help prevent pollution. By vermicomposting organic materials, those items do not end up in a landfill and create harmful methane gasses. In addition, compost also prevents pollutants found in stormwater runoff from reaching water resources.

Other than ecological benefits, composting, and specifically vermicomposting, is economically beneficial. Using compost reduces the need and subsequent costs for pesticides and fertilizers while limiting water usage. Vermicompost is a marketable commodity and a cost-effective alternative to artificial soil amendments and landfill covers. On a larger scale, by keeping organic materials from municipal landfills, composting can extend the life and usefulness of those landfills. Vermicompost, in particular, provides a cheaper alternative to the conventional methods of cleaning soils that have become contaminated by industrial waste such as oils.

For the Love of Worms

There are a variety of composting options, all of which are beneficial and will be discussed further in Chapter 1. For the purpose of this book, however, our composting journey will focus on **vermicomposting**. The process

of using worms as a viable form of composting mimics nature's inherent process of converting organic waste into a valuable product that provides the soil with depleted nutrients. The reader will learn the details on:

- Various composting methods

- An overview of the composting process

- The benefits of worms in the garden
- The life cycle and anatomy of worms
- How to set up and maintain a worm-composting bin
- Common problems in the worm bin and how to remedy them
- Other critters that might move into the worm bin
- How to use the resulting compost or vermicompost
- The process of turning vermicastings and worms into a potential business

By the end of this book, you will have gained a new appreciation for worms and their dirty work, while having fun along the way with some family-friendly activities.

CHAPTER ONE

The Vermicomposting Cycle Versus Traditional Composting – A Quick Overview

"Worms are the intestines of the earth."

~ ARISTOTLE

The origins of composting are as muddied as the garden after a downpour. Perhaps, it began when humans began to cultivate food crops in order to supplement food-gathering and hunting practices. It has been theorized that humans might have noticed crops grew better in locations where animals left waste. This theory surmises that manure might have been the first form of composting practiced by humans.

Other places in documented ancient history point to cultures having had a word for compost in their vernacular. The Greeks, Romans, Israeli Tribes, and places in the Bible all refer to natural fertilizers being used in the cultivation of crops. Fertilizers created through the composting process mentioned included manure, blood, straw, and ash from fires. Crushed bones, lime, and waste wool are later mentioned in Arabic writings from the tenth century on. The monks of the Middle Ages documented monastic use of compost in their enclosed gardens as well. Renaissance literature is laden with references to compost. Native Americans used fish bones and remnants as a compost to fertilize their crops. European settlers to America also noted the use of composting in various forms.

Compost in recent history has been used on the North American continent by both Native American tribes and, subsequently, by European settlers. Composting needs and methods have taken on a variety of forms over the years. Through centuries of trial and error, various composting practices have been used, abandoned, and revisited as viable forms of fertilizing to recycle and produce high crop yields. The recent atmosphere of being sensitive to the ecosystem has brought the focus back to organic methods of composting. Compost is more than just a fertilizer. Composting, in addition to being beneficial in the garden, is also thought to be a valuable form of recycling. Composting plays a vital part in the cycle of life and is a miniature replica of the life and death process.

As a form of recycling, composting provides the opportunity to dispose of organic waste biologically. Compost recycling makes huge leaps toward conserving energy, controlling waste, and enhancing the health of our food supply. Composting builds and rejuvenates soil quality. A variety of composting methods make composting a practical and viable practice for almost anyone.

What Happens in a Compost Bin?

Composting is the process of converting organic matter through decomposition into a useful byproduct. Composting can occur naturally or be fostered through human intervention. The process of decomposition in nature occurs at a variety of levels. To enhance this natural process, composting can be monitored carefully in a controlled environment with much success. Composting cultivates reclamation, recycling, proper treatment, and disposal of waste to save and reuse natural resources. A common understanding is that organic matter is melded together in a pile or bin, and decomposition just "happens."

Not quite. Although it does occur naturally, the composting process actually involves a series of actions accomplished by the interconnected relationships of various organisms. A more complex definition of composting than the earlier one is the oxidative

Compost bin

biological decomposition of organic materials in which organic waste is reduced to smaller volumes of materials that continue to decompose slowly, which results in balancing the carbon ratio to other elements to provide needed nutrients to plants.

To better comprehend the scientific definition of composting, it is helpful to have a basic understanding of the organisms involved and their basic functionality. The organisms within the decomposition progress are classified based upon their various functions. There are first-order consumers, second-order consumers, and third-order consumers. First-order consumers feed directly on decaying animal and plant materials. Second-order consumers feed on the first-order, and third-order feed on second order.

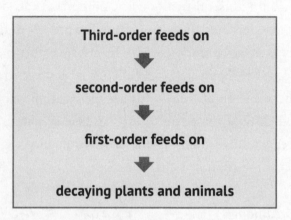

The "pecking order" system of microbial decomposition keeps the various organization populations in check. This ensures one population does not increase too rapidly and disrupt the process.

The various organisms found in the compost pile also can be classified by their functions. There are chemical and physical decomposing organisms. **Chemical decomposers** are considered microscopic organisms, such as bacteria, fungi, protozoa, and antinomycetes. The not-so-microscopic organisms, such as worms, snails, beetles, centipedes, and even mites, are classified as **physical decomposers**. Bacteria are the toughest workers of the chemical decomposers while worms are the strongest team member of the physical decomposers. Both teams assist the decomposition process by using both carbon and nitrogen within the compost materials as a fuel, along with oxygen and water to produce carbon dioxide and heat to create nutrient-rich compost, or humus.

Definitions:

Bacteria are microorganisms that are generally one-celled and can exist either independently or be dependent on another organism for life.

Fungi are parasites that feed on dead organic material and reproduce by means of spores.

Protozoa are single-celled organisms that only can be divided with the help of a host.

Antinomycetes are rod-shaped members of the bacteria family.

The breaking down of organic matter is consummated through a sequence of microorganism activity. Each microorganism reaches its optimal population when the conditions within the compost pile are "just right." The physical decomposers, such as beetles and worms referred to as first consumers, do the majority of the initial breakdown of organic waste into smaller particles. The second consumers are the bacteria, fungi, protozoa, and antinomycetes that step in next to initiate the composting process and begin to create heat. These microorganisms are considered mesophilic (work at a certain temperature) and work best at temperatures between 10 and 45 degrees C (50 and 113 degrees F).

As the temperature within the compost pile increases based on the resulting oxidation process, the next level of microorganisms step in (third consumers). Referred to as thermophiles, these guys operate best at temperatures between 45 and 75 degrees C (113 and 167 degrees F). The compost reaches this temperature within a 25- to 72-hour period and remains at that level for several weeks. This period is considered the "active" stage of the composting process.

The increased temperature within the pile kills off weed seeds and other pathogens. Throughout this active stage, the compost needs to receive a constant supply of oxygen to keep the process going. Mixing or turning the compost pile adds oxygen, also called aerating. Once the active phase slows down, temperatures decrease and the mesophilic organisms get to work again to further decompose and convert the organic material to humus, or finished compost.

The rate of composting, or how fast organic waste is converted into humus, can be affected by a variety of factors. When the composting conditions are controlled rather than occurring in a natural state, the process is hastened and yields a superb finished product. The key considerations in creating good quality compost include moisture content, aeration, temperature, and a proper nutrient balance of carbon to nitrogen. To avoid health risks associated with toxic compounds, the organic waste used for composted should be free of any pharmaceuticals, chemicals, detergents, and other harmful substances.

Overall, the composting process is a somewhat complex progression that occurs naturally and can be sped up with controlled conditions. The natural decomposition process is an effective way to reuse and recycle organic waste. Within the compost pile, hundreds of organisms work together and thrive at varying points in the composting process. Worms play a major role in the natural process and create an excellent form of home composting. Because each type of organism, including worms, thrives on special conditions and different foods, or organic materials, understanding this process and how the "pecking order" works will help the composter create the ideal product, or compost, in the fastest manner possible.

How Vermicomposting Differs from Other Forms

A sizeable portion of waste produced in the United States is organic material that can be recycled through the process of composting, which offers a host of benefits to households, institutions, and businesses. Composting daily waste items, such as food scraps and yard materials, is a cost-effective method to reducing the amount of waste in landfills. Creating a compost pile is cheaper than bagging and transferring household waste to a transfer or garbage facility. Feeding your kitchen and yard scraps to worms requires little effort. Not to mention the fact that vermicomposting also creates an excellent soil amendment used in a variety of gardening and landscaping applications. Vermicomposting returns organic, healthy matter to the soil, which, in turn, creates more nutrient-rich soil, healthier plants, cleaner air, and positively affects our health.

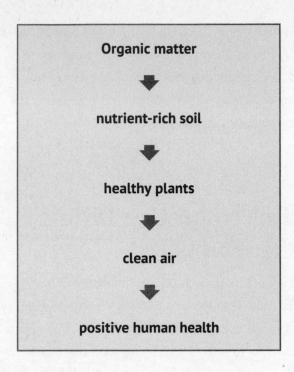

Yard waste that includes grass clippings, fallen leaves, and spent garden plants are some of the items that can be composted at home. Kitchen scraps can be composted as well. Composting can be done indoors or outdoors. It can take on a variety of forms from the simplistic to the advanced. Composting systems can have no startup cost or can be a costly investment. Types of composting systems include: vermicomposting, the focus of this book; on-site composting; in-vessel composting; turned composting; and static pile composting. Each method results in similar benefits but offers its own positives and negatives.

The Super Hero Characteristics of Compost

Compost has the power to:

- Reduce the need for dangerous chemical fertilizers
- Single-handedly suppress plant disease and pests
- Enhance agricultural crops
- Remove damaging waste products from the soil
- Destroy volatile organic compounds (VOCs) in contaminated air
- Revitalize and clean up contaminated soils in a cost-effective manner
- Facilitate reforestation and restore wetlands
- Create a barrier to remove oil, grease, heavy metals, and other solids from stormwater runoff to prevent polluted waterways

Vermicomposting

Vermicomposting is a method of composting that uses an army of workers — red worms. For this method, worms are placed in a bin along with organic waste. The worms, in turn, work hard to break down the matter into rich compost referred to as **castings**. Worm bins can be purchased ready-made or are easily constructed. These bins can be a variety of sizes to accommodate a small or large amount of organic waste. Worms, however, should not be added to an existing compost pile. Instead, a separate bin should be created for vermicomposting. The high temperatures naturally created in a regular composting bin will harm and even kill off the worms.

Fun Fact:
Cleopatra considered earthworms sacred. She banned farmers in Egypt from removing them from the soil.

Worms enjoy munching through a variety of organic waste including food scraps, plants, leaves, and even paper. Vermicomposting is an ideal composting method for homes, apartment living, and even small offices. It also makes a great program to use in schools, as children will enjoy learning about the benefits of recycling through composting with worms.

Temperatures, however, need to be considered with worm composting. Worms are sensitive creatures and can be affected by changes in climate. Worms will not do well in direct sunlight. Therefore, vermicomposting bins in dry, warm climates will need to be located in shady areas or even indoors. Likewise, if the worms are in too cold of an area, they can freeze and die. The ideal temperature conditions for worm compost bins is somewhere between 55 to 77 degrees F.

Worms will require the proper conditions and adequate food to remain alive and be productive. The basic equipment requirements for vermicomposting include worms, a bin to properly contain the worms and organic waste, and worm bedding, such as shredded newspaper or cardboard. Worm composting bins require a minimal amount of maintenance procedures including the preparation of worm bedding, burying garbage, and separating the worms from their castings. Worm compost bins can be maintained indoors or out, as long as the climate conditions mentioned above are taken into account.

Generally, 800 to 1,000 worms, the equivalent of one pound of worms, can eat and process up to a half a pound of organic waste a day. Usable worm castings take about three months to be produced. Once harvested, castings can be used as fertilizer in the garden or as potting soil. In addition, vermicomposting produces worm "tea," which is used in its liquid form as a fertilizer for plants. *Worm tea will be discussed further in Chapter 9.*

Backyard or on-site composting

Residents and small businesses generally use **on-site composting**, also referred to as backyard composting. This method is ideal for those who generate small amounts of waste because the process can be done on-site with minimal effort. For this method, yard trimmings and food scraps are the main composting agents. Animal byproducts and large quantities of food scraps, such as those produced by restaurants or hospitals, should not be used in this method due to the volume of unprotected waste that might attract unwanted visitors.

Generally, backyard composting does not require a lot of effort and does not need a lot of equipment to get started. With a little research, homeowners can get started almost immediately with backyard

composting. Backyard composting setups range from a simple pile in which to gather composting waste to more elaborate setups that include fencing to contain the waste. Backyard composting does not require constantly controlled environmental conditions, such as temperature, moisture, and aeration.

Backyard composting generally is not affected by seasonal and climate changes due to the diminutive level of organic waste. Considerations, however, will still need to be taken into account for particularly rainy or hot season changes. These considerations require only slight adjustments. Food scraps used in backyard composting sometimes can cause odors and might attract unwanted guests if not properly managed.

The results of a backyard compost pile, however, might take up to two years. Vermicomposting, as a comparison, will give you results in a few short months. Also, converting organic material to compost can take a considerable amount of time. Luckily, this process can be sped up by three to six months through manually turning the pile. The compost that results from backyard composting is an ideal fertilizer for home gardens and lawns to replenish nutrients. This compost, unlike vermicompost, is not recommended for use in houseplants due to the possible presence of weed and grass seeds.

In-vessel composting

In-vessel composting is a method by which organic waste is placed into contained equipment such as a silo, drum, or concrete-lined trench. The composting container, in this case, usually has a means by which to turn the waste material for proper aeration. Vermicomposting could be considered a form of in-vessel composting that requires less work. In-vessel composting requires close monitoring and controlling of environmental factors, such as temperature, moisture, and aeration.

In-vessel composting containers can be small or large. This method of composting has the ability to process large amounts of waste in a relatively small space. Schools, restaurants, and even larger food processing plants use this form of composting along with home composters. In-vessel composters are acceptable to almost any type of organic waste. For example, animal manure, large food scraps, and even meat can be incorporated into in-vessel composting practices. In-vessel composting is not easily accessible to animals and does not emit large amounts of odor, which is why small amounts of meat are okay to compost through this method.

In-vessel composting practices, such as vermicomposting, are not affected by climate or season changes and can be used year-round. The environment of in-vessel composting is controlled and monitored carefully. This method even can be used in freezing weather conditions with the proper insulated equipment or by moving the vessel indoors, similar to vermicomposting. Luckily, in-vessel composting produces minimal amounts of odor due to the containment of its contents and regular monitoring of its environment.

On the downside, in-vessel composters can be a costly investment compared to the minimal cost of backyard composting piles and vermicomposting. Some in-vessel composters include mechanical controls, which might require a steep learning curve and technical assistance to operate properly. On the other hand, this method, like vermicomposting, uses less land and manual labor than backyard composting piles.

With this method, the conversion process of organic waste to compost only takes a few weeks. The compost itself, however, once removed from the vessel, will need an additional few weeks to a month for the pile to cool and microbial activity to level off, unlike vermicomposting, which can be used immediately.

Turned composting

Turned composting also is referred to as the windrow method. Organic waste is collected and formed into long piles, or rows. These rows are ideally 4 to 8 feet in height and between 14 and 16 feet wide. These piles are called "windrows," and their size allows for a pile large enough to generate heat and maintain temperatures while being small enough to allow oxygen flow to their core. The piles require aeration, which is done by periodically turning the piles either manually or mechanically.

The turned compost method is ideal for large amounts of generated organic waste created by entire communities, restaurants, cafeterias, local governments, etc. This method is on a much larger scale than a vermicomposting system. Diverse wastes including yard trimmings, liquids, fish and poultry byproducts, and even grease can be used in this method. The catch is that frequent turning and careful monitoring are necessary to make this a successful composting practice.

If windrows are located in a warm, dry climate, they might need to be covered or located under a shelter in order to prevent evaporation that can dry out the piles. In rainy seasons, however, the piles will need to be made into peaks so excess water runs off and is not collected within the piles. Due to the heat generated in the core of a windrow, about 140 degrees F, windrows can be located in cold climates. The outside of the piles might freeze, but due to the heat generated, the core will remain warm.

On the negative side, windrows composting on a large scale might contaminate local ground water supplies. **Leachate** is the name of the liquid released during the composting process. Leachate can contain harmful bacteria and other substances that are leached from the compost into a liquid form. This liquid can flow into groundwater supplies and contaminate it. On a small-scale, the bacteria leached is not usually a concern, but on larger scales, such as through windrows composting, they can be harmful.

Due to its large size and contamination concerns, windrow composting might be subject to environmental regulations, unlike a home vermicomposting system. Additional requirements for large scale turned composting might  include regular testing of samples in a laboratory, being able to control odors, and adhering to zoning regulations in your area. Windrow piles also might attract unwanted animals.

Windrow style composting requires large amounts of land, good equipment for turning, continual labor to maintain, and a lot of patience. Because of all the hard work required, this composting method will create a significant amount of compost. If you are just looking for enough compost to support a small to large home garden, vermicomposting is a better method.

Static pile composting

As opposed to the rows of turned pile composting, static pile composting is in one large pile. In order to aerate the pile properly, layers of loose agents, such as shredded newspaper or wood chips, are layered in between organic waste, similar to creating "bedding" in a vermicomposting pile. These piles sometimes are placed over a network of pipes that add air in or draw air out of the pile. Larger quantities of yard waste, food scraps, and paper products work well in this composting method. Animal byproducts and grease should be avoided in static composting piles as the smell will become overwhelming and attract a host of curious animals. This method is ideal for farms, schools, or local governments. For smaller quantities of scraps, such as those produced by a single household, vermicomposting is a better method.

In warm, dry areas, static piles might be covered or placed under a shelter to avoid drying out. In colder climates, static piles might be placed indoors with proper ventilation to avoid freezing. This method does not require physical turning but does require careful monitoring. Monitoring will ensure the outside of the pile heats up along with its core. Bad odors might build up with this method and can be alleviated through the application of a thick layer of compost on top of the pile or using blowers and filters.

Static pile composting might require an investment in a host of equipment. Pipes, blowers, and fans that might be used can have a considerable cost. In addition, the equipment might require technical assistance. Vermicomposting, on the other hand, requires no technical assistance and is much less costly. Static piles require less land than the windrow method, but larger piles also will require a method of controlling airflow through those piles. Static piles transform organic waste into usable compost in a matter of three to six months. The compost then can be applied directly to the garden, lawn, and other landscaped areas.

Pros and Cons of Composting Methods

Method	Best suited for	Pros	Cons	Cost
On-site	Homeowners or small businesses	• Ideal for small amounts of waste • Minimal effort • Minimal equipment • Does not need control of environmental factors	• Might attract animals • Could take up to two years for usable compost	$
In-vessel	Schools, restaurants, small food production plants	• Uses almost any type of organic waste • Not affected by climate or season • Minimizes odor	• Requires close monitoring • Can be costly • Requires knowledge of mechanic controls	$$-$$$
Turned or windrow	Entire communities, restaurants, large food production plants	• Uses a variety of organic waste • Can be used in colder climates • Produces a large amount of compost	• Requires careful monitoring • Requires additional consideration in hot or rainy climates • Might contaminate water supply • Requires observance of local zoning regulations • Requires a lot of labor	$$-$$$

$ Minimal Cost $$ Moderate Cost $$$ Costly

Method	Best suited for	Pros	Cons	Cost
Static Pile	Farms, schools, local governments	• Takes large quantities of waste • Ready in three to six months	• Need to avoid animal by-products or grease • Additional considerations need to be made for climate conditions • Might require additional costs for equipment	$-$$$
Vermicomposting	Homeowners, apartment dwellers, schools	• Size is variable based on need • Great way to recycle household food waste	• Worms need proper care • Sensitive to temperature conditions	$-$$

$ Minimal Cost $$ Moderate Cost $$$ Costly

All methods of composting present a variety of pros and cons with some being more suitable for certain types of applications. Vermicomposting, however, is one of the easiest and most fun ways to compost and recycle. Although the methods of composting can vary greatly, the decomposition process is consistent across the board. Vermicomposting is not only cost-effective but also extremely easy to set up and can be done by anyone.

How Worms Turn Waste into Compost

Vermicompost is considered the great recycler, a way in which to reclaim and reuse waste. Generally, waste is disposed of through the process of burning or by creating large landfill-style piles of garbage. The use of vermicompost in the garden builds good soil structure, which, in turn, creates healthier and more productive plants. When used in a farming capacity, vermicompost recycles waste into a viable fertilizing agent for food-based crops.

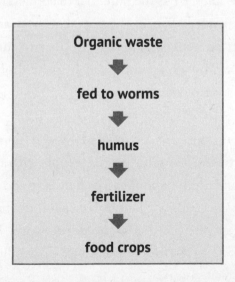

The types of organic waste that can go in a vermicompost system and other composts generally are broken down into two categories: green and brown. Some items should not be added to your compost pile. Below is general list of items for the vermicompost.

Green Material Waste	Brown Material Waste	Do NOT Use
• Vegetable peelings • Rotting fruit • Leaves • Plant trimmings • Spent flowers • Coffee grounds • Tea leaves • Eggshells	• Dried leaves • Newsprint • Dead plants • Brown paper bags • Dry grass clippings • Straw	• Dog or cat waste • Meat • Dairy • Oils or greases • Cooked foods like pasta or rice

When composted waste will be used for consumable crops, some health concerns need to be considered regarding the materials used. Manure from cats and dogs, for example, has the potential to contain harmful pathogens and needs to be avoided. When handling compost and organic waste, some people might be more sensitive than others to microbes within the materials. Proper hand washing and good hygiene should be maintained while working with vermicompost.

The high counts of the different species of molds and fungi in vermicompost can cause allergic reactions in some people. People with allergies, weakened immune systems, and asthma should avoid handling compost piles without taking the proper precautions. Dust masks, for example, can be worn to avoid inhaling spores, and gloves should be worn. If you develop an infection or have an allergic reaction because of handling compost, seek professional medical attention.

CASE STUDY:
VERMICOMPOSTING ON
A GRANDER SCALE

Kim O'Rourke
Middletown recycling coordinator
Composting Institutional
Food Scraps with Worms

245 deKoven Drive
Middletown, CT 06457
860-344-3526
kim.orourke@cityofmiddletown.com
www.cityofmiddletown.gov
Level of expertise: expert

The city of Middletown, Connecticut, received a grant from the Connecticut Department of Environmental Protection to increase recycling and encourage composting of small-scale institutional food waste. In addition to the grant, matching funds were used to set up and run a food waste vermicomposting project in the city. A greenhouse was constructed to house the worms, along with other equipment for the project. The greenhouse was chosen to shelter the worms, as it was an inexpensive way to protect the worms from the cold New England winters. Eight 4 by 8 inch wooden bins on metal frames were set up in the greenhouse to house the worms. After trying several methods, the wooden bins were the easiest method of maintaining a vermicomposting system for the city.

Over a five-year period, 8,900 pounds of food waste was collected from area restaurants, the State of CT Juvenile Training Center, a local library, Wesleyan University, a small transitional housing program, a fire department, and government offices. The project continues as more cafeterias are pursued for waste products.

In addition to the greenhouse, the project also included teacher workshops and student field trips to the greenhouse. The worms also have traveled to 30 locations, such as a variety of schools, Middletown's Open

Air Market, Russell Library, the CT Forest and Park Association, and Middletown's Sidewalk Sale for presentations and display.

"The educational component of this program has been very successful," O'Rourke said.

After the initial costs of setting up the greenhouse and equipment, the program is inexpensive to maintain. It does, however, require someone to transport food waste and feed the worms on nearly a daily basis.

According to the report, the benefits of the project include:

• Participation and education of AIC clients and staff and CT Juvenile Training Center staff in an environmental project that provides service to the community

• Reduction of wet, high-nitrogen waste being sent for disposal and therefore reduction of air emissions and ash disposal from resource recovery plants

• Increase in state and local recycling rates

• Promotion of positive relations with public/private partnerships

• The potential to expand vermicomposting services to other areas

• Use of facility for numerous educational opportunities

• Use of worms and compost in off-site demonstration and educational programs

• Support of the goals of the State Solid Waste Management Plan

For additional information on the project, contact Kim O'Rourke at the email address or telephone number above.

Why Use Vermicompost in Your Garden?

Vermicompost is nature's fertilizer. It helps plants thrive, grow, and produce. The benefits of using vermicompost in the garden are worth the effort that goes into creating and maintaining a worm farm. Worm castings, the results of vermicomposting, can create a flourishing organic garden by adding much-needed air and water to the soil as well as the three required nutrients of nitrogen, phosphorus, and potassium. Compost releases those nutrients slowly over time, which allows for better absorption through the plants. Vermicompost also suppresses disease and pests that can decimate gardens.

Earthworm Research

Two U.S. Department of Agriculture scientists, Henry Hopp and Clarence Slater, discovered the benefits of composting with earthworms in the 1940s. After finding some poor clay subsoil that contained no organic matter, the pair tried an experiment. On two separate plots, they added lime, fertilizers, and manure to produce a crop of barley and bluegrass. On one plot, they left the growth untouched. On the other, they cut the growth and used it as mulch. Then, they added earthworms to the second plot as well.

The following June, the plot without the earthworms had turned mostly to weeds, while the plot with the worms produced a large crop of barley and bluegrass. The plot with the worms was also determined to have better water-retention capabilities, a testament to both the mighty earthworm and the benefit of mulching over the winter.

CHAPTER TWO

The Gardener's Best Friend – Worms

"God gives every bird his worm, but He does not throw it into the nest."

P.D. JAMES

As a form of composting, vermicomposting offers a host of benefits. Earthworms are a natural addition to the composting process and, when done properly, can yield great results. In addition to being cost effective, composting with worms is also fun, educational, and reaps great recycling and composting results.

Fun Fact: What has no arms, no legs, no eyes, no ears, but more than one "heart?" The earthworm! It has five arteries that function as its "hearts."

Beneficial Working Worms

Like other forms of controlled composting, worms speed up and enhance the natural composting process. Worms work 24 hours a day and are often referred to as "the gardener's best friend" due to their beneficial work in the garden. Worms naturally till the garden and can aerate the soil, help fertilize the crops, eat organic waste, and naturally recondition the soil. There are also a host of other benefits to composting with worms.

Worms have the ability to convert waste naturally into simple nutrients for plants in the form of a nitrogen and phosphorus-rich organic fertilizer. Composting with worms produces this nutrient-dense fertilizer quicker than other conventional composting methods. In addition, worm compost is highly concentrated, and a little can go a long way.

Worm composting offers more options than other composting forms as it can be done either outside or inside and can be produced year-round. Because worm composting can be practiced indoors, it is a great form of composting for apartment dwellers or those with little space. In addition to the simple act of recycling household waste, the compost can be used directly in houseplants just as well as in large outdoor gardens.

If done correctly, worm composting can be virtually odorless, unlike other forms of composting. Not overloading the compost with food and keeping your food scraps fresh will contribute greatly to odor control. Proper ventilation is another factor in keeping odors down, as is limiting the amount of water in the bin.

Worm composting is an extremely affordable composting method. In fact, starting worm compost can be done with items you already have in the home. Worm composting is an easy method for children and the elderly to be involved in. The size of the compost bin can vary based on the individual need and can easily be lifted and carried around if necessary.

Five Wonderful Reasons to Make Worms your Friends

Worm compost improves your garden.

1. Composting with worms significantly reduces the garbage sent to landfills.
2. Recycling through composting helps the environment.
3. Using worm compost in the garden eliminates the need for chemical fertilizers.
4. Worm composting is easy.

CASE STUDY: LEARNING ABOUT WORMS THROUGH A CHILD'S EYES

Cynthia L. Whitaker with the help of her daughter Samantha
Psychologist and mother
Level of expertise: just learning

Cynthia Whitaker is a busy professional mother who successfully balances her work life with that of caring for her family, which includes an inquisitive, bright 3-and-a-half-year-old little girl named Samantha. In recognizing her daughter's love of the outdoors, bugs, and animals, Whitaker started an indoor worm habitat to encourage her daughter's continued learning and inquisitive nature.

"One day after fishing at our local pond, there were leftover worms. Samantha asked if we could keep them, and so our (worm) project began," Whitaker says.

They built their own worm farm by using a mixture of dirt and sand to house their worms, which they keep in the basement. The duo added the leftover fishing worms to the top of the farm and added some "food" for their new pets. Worm food in their household includes grass clippings, along with food waste.

"We enjoy watching them as they burrow into the dirt and bring the food along with them. It is always fun to go back down after we feed them to find the food gone."

Through their project, Whitaker feels that Samantha is learning all about how worms live and how they eat. The project is also helping nurture an inquisitive nature and a love of learning along with a respect for nature, values both parents work hard to strive for.

After a recent rainstorm, a few worms ended up in the family's driveway and Samantha yelled at a neighborhood child, who was about to squish one of the worms. The toddler then proceeded to rescue the worm and bring it into the "indoor basement habitat," reflecting her learning about nature and having compassion for all creatures.

Their worm project has taught Whitaker that, as parents, "We need to embrace our children's inquisitive nature and take the time to teach them and recognize that if we want our children to be active, we need to be active learners along with them."

Process of Vermicomposting

Worms have the ability to consume their own weight in organic matter each day. The product they leave behind is one of the most beneficial garden tools on the planet. In order to delve into the details of composting with worms, here are the definitions of some of the terminology used when referring to the process of worm composting.

- **Vermicastings,** or worm castings, are the byproduct, or manure, of worms that make a fabulous fertilizer.
- **Vermiculture** is the controlled method of worm farming or raising earthworms.
- **Vermicomposting** is the process of using worms to decompose organic waste and turn it into a natural fertilizer.
- **Vermicomposting system** is the term used for the worm bin and vermicomposting process.
- **Worm bedding** is the organic material used for the worms to "nest in" and start eating.
- **Worm bin** is the container that has been properly prepared for the worms to live in while they consume organic waste.
- **Worm tea** is water in which finished worm compost, or vermicasts, has been steeped to create a nutrient-rich "tea" for plants.

Worms have the seemingly magical ability to eat through a variety of organic waste and create one of the most productive composts available. Earthworms tunnel through the soil, releasing plant nutrients wherever they go. In a compost heap, worms have the ability to quickly turn it into nutrient-rich humus.

Organic waste

⬇

eaten by worms

⬇

leaves behind castings, a nutrient-rich compost

⬇

can be applied directly to the garden

Worm Compost in the Garden

Great garden soil is rich in plant-loving nutrients. A high abundance of organic matter in the soil has the ability to hold moisture while adding nutrients to the garden. Gardeners amend, or add nutrients, to the soil by means of incorporating compost. Worm compost is one of the richest forms of organic matter and can be used in the following ways:

- Mixed with potting soil for houseplants or patio containers
- Used directly in window boxes
- Sprinkled directly on lawns

- Used as mulch in garden beds
- Added directly to the garden

Worm compost is an ideal fertilizer because worm castings are close to neutral in pH regardless of the type of soil the worm ingested. Earthworm castings help to neutralize soil pH by adding calcium carbonate to the soil. Castings are also rich in minerals and nutrients that are needed by plants such as nitrogen, magnesium, potassium, and phosphorus. In addition, worm castings provide a food source for other helpful microorganisms that facilitate the composting process.

An excreted casting is about 70 percent organic matter, or humus. Soil that is laden with humus can absorb and retain water better, is loose, and does not become compacted easily. Mucus membranes secreted by earthworms maintain the nutrients in the vermicastings. The nutrients are released slowly to the plant over time and supply a continual stream of nutrition.

When set up and functioning, your vermicomposting system will generate buckets of vermicompost laden with humus, worm castings, and decomposing matter. All of these features will add much-needed nutrients to the soil. Unlike commercial fertilizers, vermicompost will not "burn" the plants. "Burning" is caused by the chemical salts in commercial fertilizers and is the process of deteriorating the plant material (leaves, flowers, etc.), giving them a "burnt" appearance. Commercial fertilizers are washed away more easily below the level of the plant's root system. Because of this "washing away," commercial fertilizers need to be applied more often and end up costing more.

Disadvantages of Commercial Fertilizers

As the topic of commercial fertilizers has cropped up, let us take a moment to discuss them in further detail. A **commercial fertilizer** is defined as a fertilizer that is manufactured chemically. In other words, it is not a naturally derived fertilizer like manure or vermicastings. Sometime in the late 1800s, commercial fertilizers were developed to aid in the mass-production of crops. During this time, agriculture morphed from a means to feed one's own family into a commercial enterprise to feed the masses. About 100 years later, according to data from the USDA, commercial fertilizer use averaged around 47,411,166 tons/year in the late 1900s.

Spraying commercial fertilizer on rice crops

Ammonium sulfate, ammonium nitrate, calcium nitrate, and sodium nitrate were among some of the first chemical fertilizers being used on agricultural crops. Ammonium sulfate, for example, was a byproduct of coal gas manufacturing. Ammonium nitrate, on another hand, was the principal ingredient used in explosives and came into vogue around the time of World War I and throughout the end of World War II. An inorganic form of nitrogen, ammonium nitrate, still is used heavily in commercial farming today.

Commercial fertilizers are manufactured today for use in large-scale and small-scale farming applications and are readily available at garden centers and home improvement stores. With the ease of use and widespread availability, why should you choose an organic fertilizer such as worm compost over a commercial fertilizer? Here the top three disadvantages of commercial fertilizer to consider:

- If commercial fertilizers are applied too heavily, toxic concentrations of salt in the soil will build up and create large chemical imbalances. These imbalances will do more harm than good to the soil and have a negative impact on the plants.

- Commercial fertilizers that contain high amounts of nitrogen are easily washed below the plant's root system, which means the plants do not receive the much-needed nitrogen for proper growth.

- Burning, as discussed earlier, can occur due to the chemical salts in the fertilizer.

FAMILY ACTIVITY:
Getting Dirty

Inquiry: Why does dirt help plants grow?

Materials needed: For this activity, you will need a package of seeds (sunflowers work well for this project), a bag of nutrient-rich garden soil (available at a local garden or home center), a bag of sand, six small paper cups, small milk cartons, or juice boxes (thoroughly washed out and dried with the tops cut off), a plastic tray or tin pan to put the cups in, spoons to scoop dirt, permanent marker to write on the planting container, water, pencils, and your binder or notebook.

Project plan: To determine if seeds grow better in nutrient-rich soil or sand that is devoid of nutrients, plant the following:

1. Using the permanent marker, mark three of the cups with the letter "N" for nutrient-rich soil and three of the cups with an "S" for sand.

2. With the spoons, fill the three cups marked "N" with the bagged soil and the three cups marked "S" with the sand, leaving about a half inch near the top of each container.

3. Place one sunflower seed in each of the six cups. Top each cup off with soil or sand, depending on the cup, to cover the seeds.

4. Put the cups on a waterproof tray like a plastic food storage cover or tin baking pan and place them in a sunny window.

5. Water the seeds on a regular basis. Be careful to not let them dry out or get too much water. The tops of the cups should be moist, but not wet.

6. Keep notes on how quickly the seeds begin to grow and draw pictures of the seedlings as they emerge.

Questions to consider:

1. Did the seeds grow in both the nutrient-rich soil and the sand?

2. If not, which one did they grow in?

3. How do the seedlings look? Are they healthier in one type than the other?

4. Why do you think the plants might have grown better in one type versus the other?

What we learned: Make a list of the things learned through the activity.

Additional reading materials: Dirt: The Scoop on Soil by Natalie M. Rosinsky (Picture Window Books, July 2002). Includes experiments to learn why dirt is important to plants and the other critters that live in the soil.

CHAPTER THREE

Getting Started – Setting up the Worm Composting Bin

"I must own I had always looked on worms as amongst the most helpless and unintelligent members of the creation; and am amazed to find that they have a domestic life and public duties! I shall now respect them, even in our Garden Pots; and regard them as something better than food for fishes."

JOSEPH HOOKER, 19TH CENTURY BRITISH BOTANIST

Worm composting begins with a container filled with bedding and red worms. *Specific types of worms will be discussed further in Chapter 4.* Food waste is added and, in conjunction with microorganisms, the worms chew through the bedding and food waste to turn it into compost. Worms can be farmed nearly anywhere. From large bins in sheds to small plastic buckets, worms can thrive if given the proper conditions. Regardless of size, one of the key components in setting up a worm bin is proper aeration, or airflow. This chapter details how to set up a worm composting bin, or vermicomposting system. The basic vermicompost system comprises five basic components:

1. A containment unit, also referred to as a bin or container

2. The worms and their biological friends

3. A controlled environment with considerations for temperature, moisture, ventilation, and acidity

4. Proper maintenance procedures that include changing worm bedding, burying garbage, and the process of separating worms from their castings

5. Procedures for using the worm castings, or worm manure

What Do You Put the Worms In?

A worm bin, referred to as a vermicomposting system if you want to impress your friends, is a compost pile in containment. Worm bins are available for purchase or can be made with simple materials. They can be made of wood, metal, plastic, or even Styrofoam™. An ideal worm bin provides darkness for the worms to do their work and can conserve moisture. There are a variety of worm bin styles of varying shapes, sizes, and materials.

Worm bin shape

Worms require a high level of oxygen. To ensure proper oxygen flow, your worm bin will need to have holes as well as be shallow to allow for proper air exchange. A good worm bin is shallow, no more than 12 to 18 inches deep. Worms feed upwards, nibbling as they go. By keeping the bin shallow, it allows for more surface area in which to nibble. In addition, bedding can get packed down easily in a deep container. When bedding gets packed down too much, it can begin to smell due to lack of proper air circulation. Lack of proper air circulation also will reduce the amount of available oxygen required by the worms and other microorganisms needed to create the compost.

Worm bins can be any shape as dictated by the space available. The important thing to remember when determining the size of your worm bin is to choose one that has a larger surface area and is not more than 12 to 18 inches deep.

Worm bin size

To determine what size bin you need, the first step is to consider the types and amount of waste you will be composting. For example, will you be composting only food scraps? Or, will you be adding yard waste as well? A good way to determine how much waste you will be adding to your worm bin is to track what you plan to add to the bin for an entire week and weigh it.

A good general rule to by is for every 1 pound of waste per week, you will need one square foot of bin space. For example, if your household only generates one pound of organic waste per week, your worm bin only needs to be 1 foot high by 1 foot wide by 1 foot long. Ideally, you should track your waste over several weeks and average the amount as waste generated probably varies from week to week. The key to an effective worm bin is based on surface space. What that means is that a good worm bin should be relatively shallow to provide more surface space for the worms. Worms will need some room to move around in to do their jobs properly without being overcrowded. One to two pounds of worms are ideal for one square foot of bin space. Another key consideration is ensuring all the worms in the bin have enough food to eat, or they might escape and look for it elsewhere.

FAMILY ACTIVITY:
Reduce, Recycle, Reuse

Inquiry: How much organic kitchen waste does your household generate in a week?

Materials needed: For this activity, the following items are needed: a bucket with a cover, a scale to weigh the bucket and its contents, a calculator, pencils, your binder or notebook, and organic kitchen waste.

Project plan: For one full week, collect all of the organic kitchen waste your household generates with these easy steps:

1. Use the scale to weigh the bucket while it is empty. This is so that the weight of the bucket is not factored into how much waste is generated. Write that number down in your binder or notebook so you do not forget it by the end of the week.

2. Place the bucket on the counter or under the sink in the kitchen. A cover will help limit flies and other pests from finding the food scraps.

3. For one full week, add organic kitchen waste to the bucket. If you run out of room, add a secondary bucket (do not forget to weigh it). Organic kitchen waste includes coffee grinds, tea bags (without the staples), vegetable and fruit peelings, uneaten fruits and vegetables from the dinner plate, scraps of bread crust, plain rice or pasta, paper coffee filters, eggshells, and even old flower arrangements that might have decorated the kitchen.

4. At the end of the week, weigh the full bucket again and subtract the weight of the bucket from step one. This will be the number of pounds your household generated in organic kitchen waste in one week.

Questions to consider:

1. Was the amount of garbage collected more or less than you expected?

2. What would the amount of kitchen waste be for an entire month? (An easy way to get a rough idea would be to multiply the number you got by four.)

3. What would it be for an entire year? (You can multiply the month number by 12 for a quick answer.)

4. Imagine if every household in your town, state, country, and the world produced that much organic garbage in one year. What would happen if that garbage ended up in a landfill? What would happen if it was recycled and reused, instead, through composting?

What we learned: Make a list of things you learned through this activity along with any other questions you might want to research about recycling and reusing organic waste.

Additional reading materials: Head to the library or bookstore to read a title that compliments this activity, *Compost Stew* by Mary McKenna Siddals (Tricycle Press; March 23, 2010). The book is an A-Z of rhyming lines of compostable items from apple cores to zinnias and everything in between. It offers a good overview of organic garbage items that can be recycled through composting.

Types of worm bins

A variety of worm bins are on the market for those who want to purchase one already made. The majority of them are fabricated out of a lightweight plastic and can be moved easily from one location to another. Complete systems that include bedding material are also available and provide for a quick startup. Complete systems do tend to be more costly, however.

Stacked plastic tray systems are one of the most popular worm bins available. This type consists of a series of stacked trays through which the worms eat upwards from the bottom as they climb from tray to tray. The process starts by adding worms and organic matter to the bottom tray. Once the bottom tray has been converted about halfway into compost, additional matter is added to the next tier up to encourage the worms upwards. Once the second tier is halfway converted, additional material is added to the third tray and so on. Once the worms reach the top and the top tray is converted into compost, the bottom tray is ready for harvesting. Once the vermicompost is harvested, the bottom tray goes on the top and the process begins again. The major benefit of this type of system is that you are able to produce a usable product in an efficient and simple manner. Not to mention it is clean and organized, and the worms and compost are contained neatly in one small area with little maintenance.

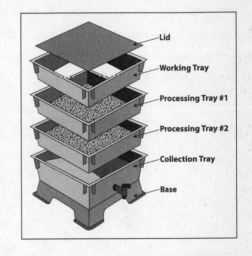

Other options include metal bins. The benefit of metal bins over plastic bins is that they are more efficient rodent deterrents. Metal bins generally are made with 26-gauge galvanized steel. Deterring rodents is not usually a big problem for bins that are kept inside the home, but they can become a problem in bins located outside or in a location where there is already a rodent problem. Other than being better at deterring rodents, metal bins have the same benefits of a stacked plastic bin system.

Bin inserts are another possible option in setting up a vermicomposting system. Bin inserts are available at home centers and fit directly into plastic storage bins. Inserts come in a variety of sizes, cost less than an entire vermicomposting system, and are simple to install. *See Appendix A at the end of the book for a buying guide.*

CASE STUDY: EXPERT HOME VERMICOMPOSTER

Dan Coulton, home gardener
Arlington, Massachusetts
dancoulton@yahoo.com
Level of expertise:
vermicomposting expert

Dan Coulton is a home gardener who is no stranger to using the benefits of compost in his gardens. For example, he compiles grass cuttings, fall leaves (specifically maple), and food scraps to create 9 by 9 foot compost squares about 3 to 4 feet high, which he rototills about once a month until the first New England frost. When spring comes, Coulton rototills the compost piles throughout early spring until he is ready to add the compost, along with manure to his garden. He then works the compost and manure deep into the soil before the first planting.

Coulton is also passionate about vermicomposting. After working with worms for the past four years, he is an expert in setting up, caring for, and using the output from his home vermicomposting system. In fact, he is considering increasing production to extend beyond his personal garden needs to be able to sell castings and worm tea at local farmers markets in Massachusetts next spring.

Rather than purchase a ready-made worm bin, Coulton created his own home system with 18-gallon Rubbermaid storage bins. He drilled holes for aeration in the bottom of the top bin and layered one bin on top of the other. In addition to allowing air to flow between the layers, the holes also allow leachate to drain down into the bottom bin.

Coulton feels that the standard 1,000 worms that most home vermicomposters start their bins with are inadequate to produce a decent amount of castings for the garden. Not to mention, they are slow to reproduce. Instead, he says to spend the money and buy 2,000 to 5,000 worms to set up a more productive system.

Some challenges Coulton has run into in his home system include unwanted critters like fruit flies. To get rid of fruit flies, he suggests putting "apple cider vinegar in a jar with foil on top" near the bin. The flies are attracted to the vinegar and are caught in the jar.

According to Coulton, worms do not actually eat garbage; they eat the microbes that break down garbage. With that in mind, he feeds his worms materials that break down quickly, such as lettuce, cucumber, zucchini, and fruit scraps (but not banana skins).

In addition to using his vermicompost to make compost tea for his gardens, Coulton also uses vermicompost as a top dressing to complement his other compost practices and as a soil enrichment for seedlings. He says he takes it one step further by using the castings in aerated compost or casting tea that increases the amount of microbes and can be used for watering or as a spray that works as a biofilm against bugs.

"Vermicomposting is a great way to add beneficial microbes to the soil that break down organic material and enhance growth without the use of chemical fertilizers," said Coulton.

Building Your Own Worm Bin

Premade worm bins generally cost anywhere from about $50 to upward of $200. However, a good worm bin can be made easily at home from materials you might already have on hand or by purchasing a few inexpensive items. Plastic lidded containers and wooden boxes are the most common homemade bin styles. Old refrigerators, toy boxes, and even Styrofoam ice chests have made good homes for a worm farm.

With that in mind, any container can be turned into a worm bin if you provide worms with the right conditions. Considerations will need to be taken in terms of the materials used in building your homemade bin. It is important to use materials that have not previously come in contact with or stored chemicals, as this can kill your worms before they even have a chance to get started in their dirty work. Even new plastic containers should be properly washed and rinsed before worms come in contact with them. Plastic bins will require more holes for aeration than their wooden counterparts. The following is an example of a simple plastic worm bin, as well as instructions for a wooden bin that is easy and relatively inexpensive to build. *See Appendix B for other building options.*

Plastic worm bin

For this single-layer worm bin project, you will need:

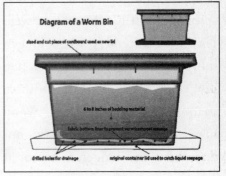

- A dark (not clear, as worms like to be in the dark) 8-gallon plastic storage container 8 to 12 inches deep with a lid

- Drill (with ¼ inch and 1/16 inch bits) for making drainage and ventilation holes

- Landscape cloth, which can be found at a hardware or garden store to fit sides and bottom of the bin

Instructions

1. Drill several 1-inch holes along the longest sides of the container and four 1-inch holes in each of the short sides.

2. Drill four to five holes in the bottom of the bin.

3. Thoroughly clean the bin with a mild soap and water. Dry the bin completely.

4. Cut two pieces of the landscaping cloth. The first should completely cover the bottom, and the second should wrap around the inside of the sides. The purpose of the cloth is to prevent the worm bedding from falling out the holes. A fine screen material also can be used.

5. Use the lid as a base to catch any excess drainage.

Wooden worm bin

Wooden bins also are constructed easily and make good vermicomposting systems as well. Plastic bins tend to last longer, however. An unfinished wooden bin can last up to two or three years with continual usage. Wood breathes better than plastic but does have the tendency to rot if too wet. A simple wooden box can be made from boards or plywood.

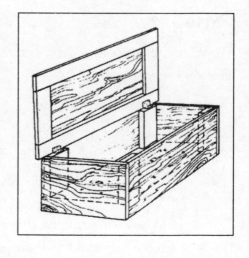

Be sure to avoid pressure-treated lumber due to the toxic elements that can leach out of the wood and harm your worms. Even an old drawer or wooden wine storage box can be used if not laden with stain or paint. Several holes will need to be drilled and landscaping cloth or fine mesh screening can be used to contain the bedding within.

This worm bin can even double as a seat.

For this project, you will need the following materials:

Materials

- One 4-foot by 4-foot non-treated ½-inch sheet of plywood
- Three 6-foot 2 by 2 boards
- One 4-foot 2 by 4 board
- One pound of 4-penny galvanized nails
- 16-inch small chain
- Two ½-inch wood screws
- Two 2-inch hinges
- Two ¾-inch wood screws
- Wood glue

The following tools will be needed for this project:

- Power or handsaw
- Hammer
- Pencil
- Square
- Tape measure
- Power drill with ¼-inch and ½-inch bits
- Sandpaper
- Proper eye and ear protection

To make the base:

1. Glue all the pieces at their joining points just before nailing for better adhesion.

2. Using the saw, cut two 23-inch 2 by 4s and two 19 ⁷/₈-inch 2 by 2s.

3. Cut a 23-inch by 23-inch piece of plywood. Nail the two 23-inch 2 by 4s to the cut plywood on opposite ends.

4. Nail the two 19 ⁷/₈-inch 2 by 2s to the remaining two sides.

5. Drill 24 to 30 ¼-inch holes in the plywood to ensure proper drainage.

To make the sides:

1. Nail the four 2 by 2s uprights to the two sidewalls along the 11 ¾-inch edge. One end of each 2 by 2 needs to be flush with the top edge of the walls.

2. Nail a 19 ⁷/₈-inch 2 by 2 hinge support to the top edge of the back wall piece.

3. Leave 1 ½ inches on each side for the 2 by 2 uprights.

4. Assemble the box by nailing the 1 ¼-inch overhang of the sidewalls to the 2 x 2s on the base.

5. Nail the front and back walls to the 2 by 2 uprights and to the 2 by 4s on the base.

6. Ensure the hinge support is located at the top of the bin.

7. Sand the inside of the box to ensure no damage will be done to your worms.

To make the lid:

1. Use a piece of 24 by 24 plywood.

2. Frame it out with 24-inch and 12 ⁷/₈-inch 2 by 2s.

3. Attach the lid to the box with the hinges. Make sure to pre-drill the screw holes into the 2 by 2 frame.

4. Attach the chain with the ½-inch wood screws.

Outdoor Worm Bin or Pit

If you live in a more temperate climate than the Northeast, you might be able to have an outdoor worm bin or pit rather than having to keep your vermicomposting system indoors. Usually, to make an outdoor bin or pit, the earth will need to be dug to a depth of 16 to 24 inches. If you wish to attempt an outdoor worm bin in a colder climate, you will want to dig deeper to avoid the freezing winter temperatures. A worm bin can be made from concrete blocks (*see the Appendix for instructions*). To create a basic outdoor vermicomposting system:

1. You will need to stake off an area about 3 to 4 feet wide and as long as you would like the pit to be.

2. Once the worm pit has been marked, remove the earth from the marked-off area and pile it off to the side. The pit will need to be a depth of 16 to 24 inches.

3. Use scrap lumber or 2 by 4s to make stakes in each of the four corners of the pit.

4. Add wire mesh at the bottom of the pit to protect the worms from moles.

5. Add boards around three sides by nailing them to the stakes. Continue stacking boards on top of each other until the height of the boards reach 32 inches (16 inside the pit and 16 inches above ground).

Like an indoor vermicomposting system, the right conditions of proper bedding, moisture levels, pH levels, and temperature will need to be observed. Outdoor vermicomposting systems do, however, require more attention than their indoor counterparts. Closer tabs need to be kept on moisture levels, pH, and temperature. Whereas an indoor worm bin is in a more "controlled" environment, outdoor bins are affected by change in weather, temperature, and other "outside" bugs that might sneak into the pile. If you live in a colder climate, the worms might not survive the freeze in the winter. Additional bedding or mulch on top of the pile will help insulate, but you will need to keep track of the temperature to ensure it does not get too cold and freeze your worms. Outdoor worm bins are not recommended for regions where temperatures consistently get below 32 degrees F.

Worm Bedding

A key component of a vermicomposting system is the **worm bedding**. In addition to retaining moisture, the bedding provides a suitable place to bury garbage and for the worms to move about. In addition to consuming the organic waste in the bin, the worms also will eat up the bedding material. Therefore, the bedding must:

- Be light and fluffy to allow for proper airflow
- Be made of a non-toxic compostable material

Proper airflow within the worm bin also will reduce and eliminate odors. A variety of bedding materials work well in a worm bin. There are advantages and disadvantages to all. Bedding mixtures also can be used, and your choice on bedding material will depend upon availability, money, and convenience.

Suitable bedding material can include shredded newsprint, fall leaves, animal manure, wood chips, coconut fiber, straw, peat moss, seaweed, and sawdust.

Newspaper

Newspaper is an ideal medium with which to create worm bedding, as it is the least expensive and is readily available. The basic ingredients used, paper and the black ink, are not toxic to worms. The color inserts should not be used in worm bedding. The pigments used in the ink for color inserts usually contain chemicals that can harm or even kill your worms. To use newspaper for worm bedding, it must be torn into strips. This can be done easily by hand. To tear up newspaper, open up a section, tear it in half by the centerfold, put one half over the other, and tear down the middle. Repeat this process five or so more times until the result is a series of strips ranging from one to three inches wide. This can be done ahead of time, and the extras can be stored for the next time the bedding needs to be changed. The newspaper bedding will need to be changed every few months.

Shredded paper

A paper-shredding machine is a great tool to create worm bedding with. Large volumes of worm bedding can be made easily and efficiently. Generally, most paper shredders make long, quarter-inch strips that retain moisture well. Newspaper and printer paper can be used for good bedding materials. Newspaper, however, does retain moisture better than printer paper. Avoid paper with inks or pigments as they might contain harmful metals or chemicals that can kill the worms. Inexpensive paper shredders are available at office supply stores.

Leaves

 Decaying leaves can create an excellent worm bed. Leaves are inexpensive and readily available in most backyards. The challenge with leaves is that they might contain other organisms that could affect the composting process, and they tend to mat together when wet.

Manure

Composted animal manures can create a natural habitat for your worms to thrive in. This form of worm bedding, however, comes with some additional difficulties. Ideally, composted cow, rabbit, or horse manures should be used, but they can be difficult to find if you do not live on a farm. The manure should come from animals that have not been on any sort of medications because the lingering effects could kill your worms. Manure is also likely to contain a host of unwanted organisms such as grubs, centipedes, or even sow worms. *Unwanted organisms will be further discussed in Chapter 7.* Setting up a worm bin with manure bedding also requires a two-step process. Manure generates a lot of heat and will need to cool for a few days before adding worms because you run the risk of killing your worms if the bedding is too hot.

Wood chips

When mixed with other forms of bedding that retain water well, wood chips can make great bedding for your worms. Wood chips are not consumed by the worms and, as such, can be reused. Not only do wood chips create air spaces throughout the bedding, they also provide bulk. Wood chips do, however, have the tendency to dry out quickly. Bedding can be created in the backyard if you have a chipper/shredder or purchased in bulk at a garden or hardware store.

Coconut fiber

Coconut fiber is a simple, clean, and easy-to-prepare medium that can be used to create worm bedding. It is available as a block of fiber that expands when water is added. It does not compose rapidly and can maintain water well. Most of the coconut fiber, also referred to as coir, on the market is actually a waste product from Sri Lanka's coconut industry. It is expensive due to distribution and export costs. Coir mixes well with other bedding and can be mixed at a ratio of one-third to the other bedding. Mixing bedding for your worms will provide a nice base for them in which to do their work and move around. Because coir can be expensive, mixing it with another more cost-effective bedding will keep your costs down.

Other bedding options

In addition to those listed above, a variety of other bedding options are available for your worm bin. Some suggestions might include straw, peat moss, seaweed, or even sawdust. Each has its unique advantages and disadvantages. To determine what works best for you, you might want to experiment with the different types of bedding to find what you have the most success with. Ideally, bedding should provide moisture, aeration, and be something readily available to you for use. If you discover that your worm bin keeps drying out, perhaps the bedding choice is to blame. Good bedding should retain water.

Bedding Type	Advantages	Disadvantages
Newspaper	• Little to no cost • Does not create dust • Readily available • Odorless	• Requires preparation time • Strips can dry out if not maintained • Can mat together, which makes burying garbage more difficult • Ink might get on your hands while working with it
Shredded Paper	• Readily available • Odorless • Clean • Easily prepared	• Requires the use of a paper shredder
Leaves	• Readily available • No cost • A natural worm habitat	• Unwanted organisms might be present • Leaves can mat together, which makes burying garbage more difficult
Manure	• Might be able to find at no cost, just the labor to haul it • A natural worm habitat • Provides a large variety of nutrients • Creates good worm castings	• May be hard to come by, depending on your location • Unwanted organisms might be present • Compacts easily • Has an offensive odor

Wood chips	<ul><li>Odorless</li><li>Clean</li><li>Creates the means for much-needed airflow</li><li>Can be reused</li><li>Mixes well with other bedding</li></ul>	<ul><li>Need to purchase or shred yourself</li><li>Dries out easily</li></ul>
Coconut Fiber	<ul><li>Retains moisture well</li><li>Odorless</li><li>Clean</li><li>Mixes well with other bedding</li></ul>	<ul><li>Not readily available</li><li>Must be purchased</li><li>Expensive</li></ul>

Additives to the bedding

Additives to the worm bedding to aid the process of vermicomposting might include soil, rock dust, powdered limestone, or eggshells. In addition to some form of bedding material, a handful or two of soil can be added to provide  some grit for the worms. **Grit** helps the worms break down food particles because worms have gizzards for stomachs and lack the normal acids that break down food particles. Soil also can add a variety of soil bacteria and fungi to get the composting process started.

Powdered limestone, or calcium carbonate, also can provide grit for the worms. One of the advantages of adding lime to the worm bin is lime helps keep the materials in the bin from becoming too acidic. If the worm bin becomes too acidic, it can kill the worms. Several forms of lime are on the market, and it is important to ensure the right one is used. Do not use hydrated or slaked lime because this will kill your worms. Pulverized eggshells will have the same benefit for the worm bin and can be used instead of lime.

Rock dust is also an effective form of grit containing trace minerals that support plant growth. Rock dust commonly is referred to as rock powder or rock flour. The construction industry creates quite a bit of rock dust through its construction processes. Rock dust might be available through local construction companies or at hardware stores and makes for an effective additive to the worm bin to enhance the vermicompost results.

Where Should the Worm Bin Go?

As when adding any new component to the garden, landscape, or home, you might be asking yourself, where should I put the worm bin? To determine the location of your worm bin, you should consider both your preferences and the needs of your worms. To make you happy, the bin should be aesthetically pleasing and convenient to use. For your worms, consider moisture, temperature, ventilation, and acidity. Worms cannot tolerate extreme heat or cold, and considerations will need to be made specific to your area for outdoor bin location. Worm bins should not be placed next to a refrigerator or anything else that might cause vibrations. Worms do not like a lot of moving around and prefer to do their work uninterrupted.

 **Fun Fact:** Worms are photophobic. This means they shun both artificial and natural light. This is why they burrow as deeply as they can to avoid light. When setting up a worm bin, it will need to remain shaded or covered for healthy and productive worms.

Personal preferences

To satisfy your requirements, your worm bin will need to be located in a convenient location for regular use and maintenance without being too obtrusive or messy. Small bins even can be kept "out of the way" under a kitchen sink yet still easily accessed for maintenance. In choosing a large worm bin that cannot be easily moved, you might want to consider putting your worm bin in a shed or basement area. Some people maintain a series of worm bins located both indoors and out.

Temperature considerations

Worms can tolerate a variety of temperature conditions but thrive and work best between 59 and 77 degrees F. Freezing temperatures might kill them, but they can survive in a basement or shed setting where temperatures reach a low of 50 F. On the other end, temperatures that reach above 85 F also can be harmful to your worms. Moistened worm bedding does offer some cooling insulation, but only by several degrees. Worm bins should not be located in direct sun, a poorly ventilated attic, a greenhouse, or a shed that not receive proper air ventilation and can heat up too quickly.

However, if your attic or shed has a means of temperature control, such as fans or a heater, this will work for your worm bin location.

 **Fun Fact:** India is the leading country in vermicomposting with an estimated 200,000 farmers practicing, according to Agriculture Business Week.

Proper airflow

Worms require oxygen for proper body functions, similar to the way we do. It is extremely important to provide for proper airflow and ventilation around your worm bin. It is not recommended to wedge your worm bin into a poorly ventilated corner or cupboard. Nor should it be wrapped in anything like plastic that blocks off the ventilation holes, as you could smother and kill your worms.

Moisture concerns

Moisture is also a key consideration when planning your worm bin. Worms require proper moisture to "breathe" through their skin. Their skin must remain moist to allow for the exchange of oxygen and for the excretion of waste to occur properly. Bedding that retains moisture is important to keeping a healthy worm bin. As bedding dries out, water can be added as needed. However, if too much water is added, it can pool and drown your worms. Placing your worm bin in a location that is accessible to adding water is key. If placing your worm bin outdoors, ensure the area does not flood.

FAMILY ACTIVITY:
Worm World, Creating a Habitat

Inquiry: How do worms live?

Materials needed: Clear 3- to 4-quart container, 1 cup fine gravel, 10 cups organic potting soil, 2 cups coarse sand, shredded newspaper, 20 earthworms, organic materials (leaves, grass clippings, food scraps), piece of cheesecloth, rubber band, dark paper, tape, water-filled spray bottle, ruler, and a magnifying glass.

Project plan:

1. Cover the bottom of the container with the gravel.

2. Add 4 cups of soil to the top of the gravel.

3. Add the sand on top of the soil.

4. Add 3 cups of soil on top of the sand and lightly mist with water.

5. Wet strips of newspaper and ring out so the paper is moist, but not soaked.

6. Neatly add the paper in a layer on top of the soil.

7. Add ½ cup of soil on top of the newspaper.

8. Add a small amount of organic matter, and cover lightly with additional soil.

9. Add the worms and observe what they do.

10. Add the cheesecloth to the top of the container and secure with a rubber band.

11. Use the dark paper to make a sleeve that can slide over the entire container and can be removed easily for observation.

12. Keep the worms in a cool, dark place.

13. Observe the worms daily, draw pictures, and take notes on what happens in the habitat. Feed them on a weekly basis by adding organic material to the top of the container and gently push under the top layer of soil.

Questions to consider:

1. What did the worms do when you put them in the container?

2. What happens to the organic matter that is added each week?

3. Did the layers of sand and soil stay even? Or, were they mixed together over time?

4. Why do you think that is?

What we learned: Draw pictures and make notes in your journal of your observations of the worms' behavior in their habitat. What did you learn about how the worms eat and make their way around their habitat?

Additional reading materials: Yucky Worms by Vivian French (Candlewick, February 23, 2010). A fictional story filled with scientific facts about how these slithery creatures move, eat, poop, and help the environment.

The Worms

"One alternative alone is left, namely, that worms, although standing low in the scale of organization, possess some degree of intelligence."

DARWIN

People mistakenly assume all worms are created equal. There are, in fact, a variety of worm species around the world. When creating a home vermicomposting system, it is important to use the right kind of worm. Worms used for composting should reproduce quickly and tolerate minimal disturbances in their containment. When small organisms are farmed in a controlled environment, they are said to be cultured. The culture, or farming of earthworms, is called vermiculture.

The worms you might find in your garden are great workers and are beneficial to the garden, but they will not be able to handle the processing of large amounts of organic matter required of composters. Worm varieties can vary amongst regions, and the type found in average garden soil is not likely the large compost-producing red worm. Red worms, a type of earthworm, are ideal candidates for the composting job.

History of the Earthworm

Earthworms generally have an unwarranted negative impression. They are referred to as "gross," "slimy," and "icky" and are generally thought to be undesirable. Earthworms are, in fact, some of the hardest-working creatures on the earth. They benefit the entire ecosystem and directly affect our food supply.

 Evolutionary theorist, Charles Darwin, studied the humble earthworm for nearly forty years. His book, *The Formation of Vegetable Mould Through the Action of Worms with Observations on their Habits*, is an unbelievably thorough resource for anything you have ever wanted or cared to know about the earthworm.

Earthworms are thought to have appeared on this planet between 120 and 600 million years ago. Currently, there are more than 6,000 documented species of the earthworm, with more being discovered and classified every year. There is even a name for the study of earthworms: **oligochaetelogy**. The earthworm used in vermicomposting is the species named *Eisenia fetida* and *Eisenia andrei*. Known as the red worm, these species are segmented worms. *This will be discussed in further detail later in this chapter.*

CASE STUDY: A SCIENCE LESSON FOR AN ELEMENTARY SCHOOL STUDENT

Abigail Shoesmith, age 6
Connecticut
Level of expertise: just learning

Shoesmith is an inquisitive little girl who has been interested in nature and all types of animals since she could talk. Growing up, she has spent time at the nearby rescue animal farm learning about all types of animals hands-on. She has gone to many museums and nature centers where she has absorbed information on a variety of topics. She also takes an active role in organic gardening at home and with her grandparents. Recently, she began to learn about recycling and its positive effects on the environment. In combining her love for nature, her inquisitive personality, and her interest in the recycling process, Shoesmith started a worm composting project at home with her family.

Shoesmith has taken an active role in learning about, setting up, and caring for the worm bin. In the process, she has acquired a lot of information on the worms, the process of recycling organic waste, and how compost works in the garden. Her journey began with reading about the worms themselves: their anatomy, their care, and even how they procreate.

While Shoesmith was waiting for the worms to arrive to fill the composting bin, she spent her time delving into a variety of books on worms. She even created her own book on worms that included drawings, the specifics on their anatomy, and details on how worms live and eat. She described how worms do not like the light and bury themselves under the ground to hide from the light. Shoesmith learned about the different types of worms, which ones are best for composting, why they were "slimy," what they liked to eat, how to care for them, how they made cocoons for babies, and how their waste was beneficial to the garden. She was surprised that worms were both male and female at the same time.

Shoesmith took great care in setting up the worms' new home in anticipation of their arrival.

Her home setup includes a three-tiered purchased vermicomposting bin located in the family's basement. Before the worms arrived, she added a combination of bagged organic garden soil with a little sand and made the worms a "bed" out of carefully shredded newspaper.

When the worms arrived, Shoesmith excitedly dug her hands into the packing material to meet her new friends. As she pulled out the worms, she began to name them before laying them gently down in their newspaper bedding in their new home. "I will call this one Wormy and this one Slimy and this one Squiggly and this one Squirmy and this one Itsy…" The list went on for quite a while before she ran out of names and decided to put the rest of her new friends in the bin at once.

Shoesmith feeds the worms on a regular basis with a variety of organic waste including food scraps and various yard materials, along with ensuring the worms are kept moist. Through her project, she has learned about the anatomy, work, and life cycle of a worm.

She also can pick out where worms have been working outside in the yard by recognizing the waste they leave behind from burrowing through the dirt.

Anatomy of Worms

Earthworms have no backbones and are classified as cold-blooded invertebrates. Their bodies are segmented into varying widths. The largest segment is at the front end of the worm. Worms are both male and female; they produce eggs in addition to sperm. *This will be discussed in more detail later on in the chapter.* Red worms, the type used in vermicomposting, reproduce quickly. The mating process produces baby worms twice as

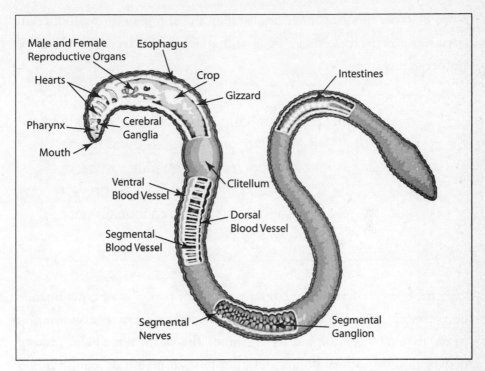

fast as normal breeding because each worm gives birth. Thus, earthworm reproduction is quick, which means more worms in your composting system.

Located approximately in the middle third of the worm's body, **between** its head and tail, is an area known as the **clitellum**. The clitellum **appears** as a band or saddle around the worm, its location varies by species, **and it** indicates that the worm is sexually mature and old enough to breed. The clitellum can appear as a swollen area and is often a different color **than the** rest of the worm.

With the exception of the first segment, the remaining segments **of the** worm have **setae**, or bristles. The setae's main function is movement, **and** they vary in length and shape by worm variety. The earthworm **extends** it body to move, anchors itself via the setae, and then contracts its **body.** This process is referred to as a step. The earthworm generally makes seven to ten steps per minute. The setae also play a vital role in the reproduction process as it helps them move along and attach themselves to the body of another earthworm.

Fun Fact: What happens if you cut a worm in half? Depending on where the worm was cut, it has the power to regenerate lost parts. The anterior end, for example, can grow a new tail. The tail, however, cannot grow or regenerate a new head.

A worm's body contains several different types of pores. Some types include the reproductive pores, spermathecal and female, as well as dorsal pores, which excrete fluid known as worm slime. The worm slime helps to keep the worm moist so it can breathe. Other pores function to remove liquid waste from a worm's body. An earthworm's body is made up of 75 to 90 percent water and ranges from an inch up to 8 inches, on average, long.

Fun Fact: The largest earthworm ever recorded measured 22 feet and was discovered in South Africa.

Worms do not seem to have a defined head like other animal species. Instead, the end with the mouth is considered the head, while the opposite end is the tail. Worms eat by picking up food in the mouth and pulling it into what is referred to as the **alimentary canal**. The canal is a tube that runs the length of the worm's body from mouth to anus. The food passes through the tube and is broken down through the varying tubal sections. The sections of the alimentary canal include the buccal cavity (a mouth without teeth or jaws), the pharynx (suction pump for food), the esophagus, the crop (stores food), the gizzard (grinds food), and the intestine (digestion and nutrient absorption). Food that is not digested or absorbed is excreted as worm castings, or manure.

Narrow blood vessels within the worm absorb nutrients that feed the rest of the worm's body. Located between the vessels in the upper part of the worm's body are a series of loops of vessels, or hearts. The number of worm hearts varies by species. Small blood vessels connect the main body parts and vascular network. The small vessels, or capillaries, bring nutrients and oxygen to the rest of the worm body while also removing waste. Worms' bodies contain red blood with hemoglobin.

An earthworm's brain is actually a mass of neurons referred to as a ganglion. It is connected to nerve cords that run the length of the worm's body. Each segment of the worm contains additional ganglia with nerve fibers running to the rest of each segment. Sensors are attached to the nerve fibers and tell the worm about its environment.

 **Fun Fact:** Earthworms cannot detect the color red.

Worms do not have lungs. Instead, they bring oxygen to the rest of their body by dissolving oxygen through the surface of their bodies. Earthworms require a lot of water to be able to take in oxygen. They use their setae to hear through vibrations. Nerve receptors detect light changes that allow earthworms to "see."

Are worms male or female? How do worms procreate?

 As mentioned earlier in the chapter, worms are both male and female and, therefore, are considered hermaphroditic. There are two male segments and one female segment in each earthworm. An earthworm is sexually mature about three to six weeks after it hatches. Its sexually maturity is signified by the appearance of the clitellum, or band that secretes mucus.

To procreate, one earthworm will position itself alongside another, head touching tale end. The worms will lie together and secure themselves to each other by the setae. The clitellum secretes mucus, which holds the worms in place. The semen of the worms passes from one to the other and is stored in the sperm storage sacs. Worm mating can take place over a span of two to three hours before the worms move apart from each other.

After mating, a cocoon is formed a few days later to deposit eggs in. The cocoon is created through secretions from the clitellum and forms in a thick, hard layer around the clitellum. The worm then moves its body and "backs out" of the cocoon. As it does this, the eggs and sperm are deposited into the cocoons. The ends seal themselves and the cocoon is formed. A varying amount of eggs are fertilized in each cocoon.

Cocoons are yellowish-white in color when first formed and slowly get darker as the embryos within them continue to grow. A cocoon is the size of a small grain of rice and is shaped like a lemon. The color changes from yellowish-white to dark yellow to light brown. When the hatchlings are about to hatch, the cocoon takes on a reddish-brown hue. It takes about three weeks before worms hatch.

Mating Process of the Earthworm

Two worms join together with mucus from their clitella.

Sperm passes from each to the sperm storage sacs in the other.

A cocoon is formed on the clitellum, or band, of each worm.

The worm then backs out of the cocoon. Eggs and sperm are deposited in the hardening cocoon as it passes over the ovaries and sperm storage sacs.

The cocoon then seals up at each end and fertilization takes place.

At least two baby worms hatch out of the cocoon.

Types of Worms Available

Earthworms are found all over the world with the exception of frozen Arctic areas and extreme hot desserts. There are thousands and thousands of worm species, each characterized by having no legs. The earthworm is a part of the genius phylum Annelida, or segmented worms. There are about 9,000 species of segmented worms. The types of worms used for vermicomposting are terrestrial earthworms, as opposed to aquatic, and fall into three groups: litter-dwellers, shallow-soil dwellers, and deep-burrowers.

Terrestrial Earthworm Types

Litter-dwellers: Live on the topmost layer, or litter layer, of the soil. These little guys are usually found under fallen leaves or needles on the forest floor.

Shallow-dwellers: Live on the top 12 inches or so of the soil and burrow randomly throughout the soil without making permanent burrows. During the cold seasons, the worms burrow deeper and hibernate to avoid being frozen.

Deep-burrowing: Build deep burrows, or tunnels, down deep in the soil, sometimes to six feet. These worms take food and drag it down into their burrows, and they provide oxygen to the soil in the process. Deep burrowers do not hibernate, but do retreat to the bottoms of their burrows during the colder months.

Night crawlers, African night crawlers, red worms, red wigglers, red tiger, and blue worms are some of the worms most commonly used in vermicomposting. Often, the worms in these categories are often referred to by the same name, red worms, as not many people are specialists in the differences between the breeds. Following is a chart listing the characteristics and uses of the worms.

African Night Crawlers

Latin Name: *Eudrilus engeniae.*

Also known as: The giant night crawler

Physical Characteristics: red with cream stripes; grows up to 12 inches long

Habitat: Shallow-dwellers; prefer to habituate in the top few inches of the soil

Loves to Eat: A diet of rich compost

Specifics: Warm temperatures; are not good in areas that go below 50 F. They make good composters but move around a lot and often climb out of the bin.

Blue Worms

Latin Name: *Perionyx excavitus*

Also known as: Indian blue and Malaysian blue

Physical Characteristics: A deep purple to dark reddish-purple; average about 6 inches long

Habitat: Litter-dwellers; like to hide under mulch. Their preferred temperature is in the 68 to 77 F range.

Loves to Eat: A diet of compost and decaying plant and animal matter

Specifics: Active wigglers; make excellent fishing worms. They also make good composting worms in warmer climates, as they do not like cold.

Night Crawlers

Latin name: *Lumbricus terrestris*

Also known as: Night walkers, dew worms, rain worms, and night lions

Physical Characteristics: A red to brown color; grow up to 12 inches long

Habitat: Deep-dwellers; create vertical tunnels up to 6 feet deep. They prefer temperatures around 50 F.

Loves to Eat: A diet of leaves and mulch

Specifics: Not good for indoor vermicomposting due to their deep borrowing nature but can be used effectively in an outdoor compost in temperate climates

Red Wigglers

Latin Name: *Eisenia fetida*

Also known as: Garlic worm, tiger worm, and manure worm, as they can often be found under large piles of animal manure

Physical Characteristics: Rust brown in color with alternating bands of yellow and maroon; can grow up to 3 inches long

Habitat: Shallow-dwellers; live in the first few inches of the soil; prefer temperatures of 59 to 77 F

Loves to Eat: Rich compost, manure, decaying animal and plant matter

Specifics: The ultimate composting worm, as they have the ability to compost large amounts of food each day. They tolerate bin life well and can accommodate well to variances in temperature, acidity, and moisture.

Red Worms

Latin Name: *Lumbricus rubellus*

Also known as: Blood worms and red wrigglers

Physical Characteristics: Dark red with a light-yellow underside; have no striping variations. They grow up to 3 inches long.

Habitat: Prefer the top 6 to 12 inches of soil and temperatures in the 64 to 72 F range and are considered shallow-dwellers.

Loves to Eat: Consume rich compost, decaying plant and animal matter

Specifics: Make good compost worms, as they aerate the soil well and are active in light. They are also great bait worms and are a preferred food for fish.

Red Tiger

Latin Name: *Eisenia andrei*

Also known as: Tiger worm or red tiger worm

Physical Characteristics: Dark reddish to purple in color; grow up to 3 inches long; might be banded

Habitat: Live only a few inches deep in soil and love conditions under the mulch pile and are considered shallow-dwellers

Loves to Eat: Love to consume manure, compost, decaying plant and animal matter

Specifics: A good worm for vermicomposting; are also used for bait as they wiggle a lot in the sun

Best Worms for Composting

In addition to breed types, there are two other options when choosing worms for your worm bin: breeders and bed-run. **Breeders** are fully mature worms while **bed-run** are worms of all ages. When starting off, you might want to choose bed-run as they adjust quicker and cost less than the breeders. Breeders are better suited once you have gained some experience working with worms. To help in the decision process, below are the characteristics of each:

Breeder	Bed-run
• Lay cocoons more quickly	• Get more worms per pound
• Increase in population more quickly	• The young worms will grow quickly and begin reproducing
• More expensive	• Adjust to the bin more quickly
• Take longer to acclimate to the bin	• Cheaper cost

How many worms do you need?

In general, worms consume half of their body weight per day. Biologically speaking, it is the weight of the worms, or **biomass**, that is the key ingredient in vermicomposting, not the actual number of worms. Teenage worms, like teenage humans, usually consume larger amounts of food than their fully mature adult counterparts. Regardless of the amount of worms you get, the population will stabilize depending on the amount of food fed to them. Reproduction will slow, and some will die off.

In order to figure out how many worms you will need to purchase for your worm bin, you will need to determine how much garbage in pounds your household produces on a daily or weekly basis. An easy way to figure out the number of pounds is to collect organic garbage for one week and weigh it to determine your daily household average of trash.

To do this,

1. Weigh an empty large container such as a bucket or rubber bin.

2. Add your household organic scraps to the bucket for a week, or seven days.

3. Re-weigh the bucket with the garbage and subtract the weight of the container from that number.

4. This is the number of pounds your household creates in waste a week. Divide that number by seven to determine how much garbage is produced on a daily basis.

5. You will need two times that number in worms to consume your garbage on a daily basis.

Worm Math

Question: The Pennington family produces 7 pounds of organic trash in one week. How many pounds of worms will they need in their vermicomposting system to consume their trash?

Formulas:

pounds of waste per week ÷ number of days in a week = pounds of waste per day

$7 ÷ 7 = 1$

pounds of waste per day × 2 = pounds of worms needed

$1 × 2 = 2$

Answer: Because worms consume half of their body weight per day, the Pennington family will need 2 pounds of worms in their bin to consume the 1 pound of waste per day.

Where do you get the worms?

Once you have purchased or made your worm bin, prepared it with worm bedding, and determined the types of worms for your system, it is time to purchase the worms. But, where does one buy worms? If you have chosen to purchase a ready-made or commercial bin, these often come with the correct number of worms for the bin. Otherwise, places to purchase worms include garden centers, bait shops, commercial worm growers, and the

Internet. In general, worms are sold by the pound. One pound of mature worms contains about 1,000 wiggly little friends.

The challenge with purchasing worms is that garden centers and bait shops generally just sell "red worms," and they often do not know the specific breed they have. Commercial worm growers will have their types of worms classified so you know exactly which worm you are getting. This ensures the conditions you set up in your bin are to the liking of your worms. Some tips on purchasing worms:

1. Ask the seller for the scientific, or Latin name, of the worm he or she is selling.

2. Do your research ahead of time so you are informed about the type of worms that will work best for your needs.

3. Know your terminology: breeders versus bed-run.

4. Worms are sold by weight: A pound will usually contain 1,000 breeders or 2,000 bed-run.

5. Have your worm bin set up and prepared before purchasing worms so you can add them right away when they arrive.

Fun Fact: More than 1 million earthworms can be found living in 1 acre of land.

FAMILY ACTIVITY:
The Anatomy of Worms

Inquiry: How are worms different from other animals?

Materials needed: A reference book on worms (information is available in this chapter; additional reference books are listed below); a couple of worms; pencils, crayons, or markers; and your notebook or binder.

Project plan: Worm bodies are very different than most animals'. Worms also make cocoons for their babies to hatch from. For a simple comparison activity, follow these easy steps:

1. Draw a picture of a dog.

2. Next to it, draw a picture of a worm.

3. For the dog, fill its eyes, ears, nose and where you think his heart is.

4. Now, can you fill in the same on the worm's body?

5. Worms make cocoons for their babies to hatch from, much like an egg. Draw a picture of a chicken egg. Next to it, draw a small worm cocoon.

6. How do you think they differ?

Questions to consider:

1. Can you tell where the worm's head is? What about its tail?

2. Does a worm have eyes or ears? Or, a nose?

3. Worms have multiple hearts; where do you think all the hearts are in its body?

4. How do you think a worm eats?

5. Did you know worms are both male and female?

6. How do you think the worm babies come out of its cocoon?

7. How many do you think come out? How many come out of a chicken egg?

What we learned: In what ways did you discover worms differ from other animals?

Additional reading materials: Garden Wigglers: Earthworms in Your Backyard by Nancy Loewen (Picture Window Books, January 2006). This book details the physical characteristics, life cycle, and behavior of earthworms and includes an anatomy diagram and activity.

CHAPTER FIVE

Caring for Your Worm Bin

"Worms have played a more important part in the history of the world than most persons would at first suppose."

~DARWIN

Most worm-bin owners will tell you that worms are easy to care for. They are simple creatures with simple needs. However, that does not mean you can neglect their care or that they will survive anywhere. To get the best-quality vermicompost and keep your worms in the best health, you will have to ensure your bin has a number of amenities if you want your worms to stay there.

Feeding Your Worms

Earthworms, like most organisms, require a balanced diet for proper functioning. Fats, proteins, minerals, and carbohydrates make up a well-balanced worm diet. Worm growers refer to the organic materials fed to worms as **feedstock**. The feedstock includes the bedding material as well as the organic waste. Home vermicomposting systems are beneficial in the reduction of household waste, and kitchen waste often contains enough of the proper diet to maintain worms in a home system. Commercial feedstock, however, is also available for purchase but is not readily available and can be costly.

Fun Fact: The natural habitat or worms varies greatly — from fields and forests to cities and farms.

Worms consume many of the items we throw in our household garbage bin. Generally, the items that fall under the organic kitchen waste and table scraps heading are the type of "garbage" worms enjoy as their meals. Food wastes might include any type of waste that is generated in food preparation. Some examples might include: potato peelings, lettuce, orange rinds, coffee grinds, and tea bags. Other items that can go in the worm bin include dried leaves, garden clippings, and some forms of animal manure.

Worms also need some form of **grit** in their diet. The bodily function of a worm includes the process of grinding up food in their gizzards. A **gizzard** is an organ found in the digestive tract of some animals that serves as a stomach to grind up foods. Grit added to a worm's diet helps the gizzard grind up foods into smaller pieces. In its natural habitat, a worm takes in soil that helps provide grit for the digestion process. In a controlled habitat such as a worm bin, grit needs to be added every few weeks or so. Grit to add to the worm bin includes: fine soil, eggshells, rock dust, and coffee grinds.

Worm Menu

- Fruits and fruit peels
- Vegetables, peels, and tops
- Coffee grounds and filters
- Tea leaves and tea bags
- Kelp
- Pasta and rice
- Melons and peels
- Flowers and stems
- Grass clippings
- Leaves, brown and green
- Eggshells
- Cereal
- Cakes
- Muffins
- Kelp
- Pizza crusts
- Composted manure from horses, rabbits, sheep, chickens, cows, or goats

What not to feed your worms

Foods such as eggs, meats, and dairy products are enjoyed by worms but are not recommended for home vermicomposting systems as they can smell and attract unwanted animals and pests to your bin. It also has been discovered that citrus products in excess can kill off worm populations in your bin. The following list contains some good guidelines of foods to avoid feeding your worms:

Non-biodegradable items: Items such as plastic bags, rubber bands, aluminum foil, glass, and sponges are not biodegradable, and the worms cannot process them.

Dog and cat feces: Disease organisms present in cat and dog feces are harmful to humans. *Toxoplasma gondii*, for example, is found in cat feces and can be transmitted through a mother to her unborn baby. It can cause brain damage.

Meat waste and bones: Decaying meat should not be used in a home bin as it can produce offensive odors and attract unwanted organisms and animals to the worm bin.

Heavily spiced foods

Hair

Dairy products: Milk, yogurt, butter, and eggs should not be included in the worm bin.

Poisonous plants

Oils

Soaps

Salt

Wood ashes

Preparing meals for your worms

Preparing meals for your worm bin is a simple process that involves saving food wastes, preparing the food, and burying the food. To save food wastes, it is easiest to collect the kitchen scraps in one central location: a plastic bucket under the sink, for example, or a bowl on the counter next to the sink. Other options to collect your kitchen scraps might include an extra trash can next to your other household trash or a plastic bag hanging by the window or on a hook. One thing to keep in mind when collecting kitchen scraps is to avoid covering your collection unit. Placing a tight lid on your container does not allow for airflow, can create unwanted odors, and promotes the growth of anaerobic bacteria. **Anaerobic bacteria** grow in environments that lack oxygen and can create an acidic product that is harmful to your worms.

The majority of kitchen wastes can be added directly to the worm bin without any preparation. It is a good idea, however, to get in the habit of washing everything, as food items often are sprayed with pesticides. Chopping or grinding food up before adding it to the bin will speed up the composting process because large pieces need to decompose for a little bit before the worms can digest them.

Worms can be fed on your timetable. Often, people feed their worms twice a week so the garbage is not sitting in their kitchen for extended amounts of time. Others feed their worms once a week when their collection bowl starts to get out of hand. Once you get used to  the process, you will find your own rhythm of feeding that works best for your household. As long as your worms are getting enough food, timing does not really matter all that much. It is not necessary to begin feeding the worms the moment they arrive. Instead, let the worms get acclimated to their new home for a few days to a week before feeding them for the first time. At this point, the worms will be well adjusted to their new home and hungry.

To put food in the worm bin, pull back the top layer of bedding and bury the food about two inches deep. Replace the bedding. By burying the food, it will control odors in the bin as well as prevent pests such as flies. Another option is to add the food on top of the bedding and add another layer of bedding on top of the food. Part of the fun of a worm bin is experimenting to discover which methods work best for you. Your worms will be getting enough food when there is a good mix of compost to unfinished scraps in the bin (50-50) on a weekly basis. If you go on vacation, just leave a little "extra" food in the bin. Worms are low maintenance and can handle slight fluctuations in food. *To determine if your worms are receiving the proper amount of food and if problems such as mold are really "problems," refer to Chapter 6 for troubleshooting information.*

Another method some worm farmers use for feeding their worms is the quadrant system. Rather than burying the food in "random" spots in the bin, a quadrant system allows you to better regulate and monitor the amount of food the worms are eating. This method works well for people who want to be more in control of the bin or for a teaching scenario, where students will need to make detailed observations and track the progress of the work in the worm bin. To use the quadrant system, divide the worm bin into four equal sections and follow these steps:

1. The first time you bury food for the worms, put it in quadrant one.

2. The next time you feed the worms (in a couple days), bury in quadrant two.

3. The following time (a couple days later), bury the food in the third quadrant.

4. Finally, bury the food in quadrant four in another two to three days.

5. Start back again at quadrant one.

1	2
3	4

The worms will follow the food from quadrant to quadrant. This method is also helpful in determining if you are feeding the worms a proper amount of food. If there is still food in quadrant one by the time you have made one full rotation, you might be feeding the worms too much or too often. If this is the case, give them a few days to finish eating what is already there before you give them additional food and starting the process again. Adjust by feeding the worms less often or by giving them less food. On the other hand, if the worms already have eaten through most of the food in quadrant three by the time you get around to quadrant one again, they may not be getting enough food. Adjust by feeding the worms more food or more often.

Bedding Requirements: Temperature, Aeration, pH, and Moisture Levels

The condition of the worms' environment is an important factor in how well your vermicomposting system functions. Temperature, acidity, aeration, and moisture are the key concerns for a healthy worm bin. Major changes in any of these conditions can lead to worm shock and often kill off huge worm populations.

The temperature of worm bedding ideally should be kept at a temperature that ranges from 55 to 77 F. If temperatures rise above 80 F or below 55 F, the activity in the worm bin will be slowed down greatly. Thermometers can be used to confirm the temperature in the worm bin. Specialized thermometers for compost bins are also available for sale. Temperatures that dip into freezing or go above 90 F will kill the worms in the bed. If you are in an area that is extremely warm or cold during any season, you will need to pay special attention to the temperature and how it affects the worm bin.

Acidity levels are referred to in terms of pH levels. A **pH level** measures the potential hydrogen, or levels of acidity to alkalinity on a scale. The pH scale is a number scale that ranges from one to 14. The lower numbers on the scale, the more acid the soil is. The higher the number is on the scale, the more alkaline the soil is said to be. The number 7, in the middle of the scale, is said to be a neutral pH. Most plants and animals require a pH range between 6 and 8, with 7 as the ideal. The pH level in the worm bin can fluctuate greatly based upon the living conditions and the food in the bin, but it should stay within the 6 to 8 range. Meters that read pH levels are available for worm bins to ensure the proper level of acidity in your worm bin. Meters can be purchased at farm, garden, and hardware stores. They also can be found online. The level should be checked every one to two weeks.

If the pH level of your worm bin is too acid, below 6, add crushed eggshells and refrain from adding acidic fruit scraps such as oranges or lemons until the pH returns to normal. If the pH level in the bin is too alkaline, or above an 8, add additional bedding such as newspapers along with citrus scraps.

In a worm bin, proper aeration, or oxygen levels, is key for the survival of the worms and their friends, the aerobic bacteria. In order for a worm to breathe properly, oxygen must dissolve in the mucus that is secreted from the worm's skin. Lack of proper oxygen will kill the worms and breed anaerobic bacteria. Odors emanating from the worm bin are an indicator of anaerobic activity and the need for additional aeration. Proper drainage holes and loose bedding are two ways to ensure proper airflow in the worm bin.

Fun Fact: An earthworm is so strong that it can move stones 60 times its own weight.

The level of moisture in the worm bin is also an important factor in the overall health of the bin. Worms breathe by taking in oxygen through their skin, which must be kept moist for proper functionality. If worms dry out, they no longer will be able to breathe and will die. Moisture levels in the worm bin should be kept at about 75 percent moist. Dipping below 60 percent can dry the worms out. Moisture meters are available as well at your garden, farm, or hardware center as well as on online. If your moisture levels are too low, you may need to change your bedding to something that retains moisture better. Or, you can spray the contents of the bin with a water mister on a daily basis. If your worms are too wet, try adding additional bedding to help absorb some of the extra moisture.

Time to make the bed (again)

Regardless of moisture levels, the worm bedding should be changed approximately every three to six months. After about three months of working away, the number of worms will be high compared to the amount of compost. Not to mention, the compost will not be quite ready. At about four months into the process, the quality of the compost will be good and the number of worms still will be considerably high. After six months, the quality of the resulting compost will be extremely good, but many of the worms will have died. With this in mind, six months is about the ideal time for changing out the bedding, as no organism does well living in its own waste. Although some of the population will tend to die off by the six-month mark, you will not want all of your worms to die from living in their own waste.

To completely change the worm bedding of a single-layer bin, follow these easy steps:

1. Lay newspaper on the surface you will be working on. Two to four full sheets should be sufficient to cover your work area and contain the contents of the worm bin. This can be done on the floor, on a table, or even outside on the lawn.

2. Gently dump the contents of the bin out onto the newspaper, being careful not to disturb the worms with any quick, sudden movements.

3. Place fresh bedding of your choice in the bin, following all the same requirements as when the bin was first set up (*refer to Chapter 3*).

4. Gently brush aside the soil from the worms with your fingers. To avoid the light, the worms will begin to move closer and closer together until they are in a big pile. This is the perfect time to collect the vermicastings and harvest any worms. *The process of both will be discussed further in Chapter 8.*

5. Return the worms to their home, along with some food, and the process will begin all over again.

To make bedding changes easier, another simple method can be employed within the worm bin. Either purchase or create a bin with a center divider. The divider should be made out of stiff plastic or some other non-decomposing material that runs the length of the worm bin. Only place bedding and worms in one half of the bin at a time. When you are ready to change the bedding, place new clean bedding with food in the empty half. Remove the divider and in about two to three weeks, the majority of the worms will have migrated over to the new half. This idea also makes it easier to remove the compost from the original half.

CASE STUDY: UNIVERSITY OF VERMONT RECYCLING MANAGER

Erica Spiegel, recycling manager
University of Vermont
284 East Avenue, Burlington VT 05405
Erica.Spiegel@uvm.edu
Level of expertise: intermediate

Erica Spiegel is a student, a professor, and the recycling manager at the University of Vermont in Burlington. Not to mention, she is also a home gardener. Erica has used vermicompost and worm castings in her vegetable garden, as a top dressing for houseplants, and as a "brew" of vermicompost tea, which she sprays on her plant leaves. Vermicomposting has helped Spiegel reduce her household trash:

"I do not put any organics or vegetative waste in my home trash at all," Spiegel said: "My home trash does not smell or have foul odors because what little trash I make is 'dry.'"

Because one box of worms is not enough, Spiegel has both an outdoor and indoor system. She also admits to keeping a worm box on occasion under her desk in her office at UVM.

"In my backyard, I have a three-bin setup made out of wood pallets," she said. "Admittedly, I do not tend to it very actively. It is what you might call a 'cold compost' system. I do not necessarily mix and balance to get the pile hot. I just pile up and add food scraps and yard waste as I generate waste, and let the pile naturally 'rot.' The downside of this is that there is not 'heat' in the pile to properly kill weed seeds that end up in there."

Indoors, in her basement, is where "the real fun happens" in a small vermicomposting box. The basement box is where Spiegel actively feeds the worms, keeps them healthy, and periodically harvests the worms and the finished castings. Harvesting the worms and the finished product can be a tedious task, she explains. Every six months or so, Spiegel uses a bright light and forms piles in order for the worms to burrow down out of the light. Then, she scoops up the finished castings. Sometimes she even screens them further. But it is worth the effort to get a fresh batch of worms and bedding started and to get finished compost, Spiegel thinks.

"In harvesting the worms, I can help friends start their own worm compost boxes," she said. "And I use the castings to fertilize my houseplants and garden (the yield is small quantity)." This is an especially nice approach during the wintertime in Vermont when Spiegel does not want to trudge through the snow to get to the backyard compost pile.

Spiegel's setup is a simple, low-tech box made out of a 10-gallon Rubbermaid® plastic tote. She drilled holes in the tops and sides and placed "mesh" over the holes to keep fruit flies away. She also drilled a drain hole on the bottom in case the bedding and materials get too wet.

At the university, Spiegel also works with a larger wooden box that students tend to. This is a "nicer box," she says, with a hinged wooden lid. Controlling moisture in the plastic box is a challenge, whereas some people prefer a wooden box that "breathes" easier. Spiegel often leaves the lid slightly ajar to let excess moisture out, or adds dry fresh bedding to compensate for moisture concerns. Preventing fruit flies is another common challenge for vermicomposters. To prevent fruit flies, Spiegel makes sure to bury any new food added to the bin completely and keeps a damp sheet of newsprint covering the top layer of bedding so the flies cannot reach the bedding.

In addition to moisture concerns and controlling fruit flies, Spiegel offers a suggestion on how NOT to accidentally cook your worms. Many books warn that the red wiggler worms used in composting need to be kept at comfortable temperature between 50 and 77 F degrees. Mary Appelhoff's book warns, "Bedding temperatures above 86 degrees F could be harmful to worms."

"Last summer, I was transporting my worm box to help a friend start a box of her own," Spiegel said. " I left the box in the back of my car for several hours. I figured I would crack the windows a bit and all would be fine. To my horror, when I opened the lid of the box there was a horrible odor — like the smell of squashed frogs on a rainy highway — and all of my worms were gone. Melted and slimy to be exact. I had accidentally 'cooked' all my worms in the heat of my car."

In learning from Spiegel's tips, she offers the following advice to vermi-composting beginners:

"Just get started! There is no need to purchase a fancy commercial worm box. You can make a simple comfortable box for your worms with items you have around your house. You can line a cardboard box with a big plastic bag to get started. Use newspaper for bedding (it is best to ma-chine shred it, or else hand shred it into small strips). You also can use autumn leaves as bedding. No need to purchase fancy special bedding (like coir), although you can if you want. Start simple … and do not be afraid about your red wiggler worms escaping. They will stay in the con-fines of their cozy worm box home."

Rotating Worms

If you plan to have more than one worm bin, either side-by-side or stacked in tiers, you may want to rotate the worms from bin to bin to make the bedding changes and harvesting process simpler. For example, when the bedding is mostly gone and the food scraps have turned into a dark, rich, soil-looking material, you can move the worms from the "old" bin to the next "new" bin. In order to do this, follow these easy steps:

1. Prepare the "next" bin by setting it up with bedding as explained for a new bin in Chapter 3.

2. Gently separate the worms from the vermicompost (the dark, rich material) with your fingers. This also can be done by gently tipping the contents of the bin out onto a newspaper and separating the worms as described previously.

3. Move the worms to their new home to begin the composting process all over again.

4. Remove the "waste" the worms left behind in the first bin and use it as compost. *This process of harvesting the compost, or vermicastings, will be discussed further in Chapter 8.*

Winter Care

Keeping a productive worm bin during the winter months does not require that much additional care. If the bin is located in a basement, garage or other location where the temperatures throughout the year remain at a constant temperature, you will not need to make any changes to the process of what you have already been doing. If, however, the bin is located where temperatures will get too low and might freeze the worms, you can take some winterizing steps before the cold sets in. An outdoor bin, for example, could be moved indoors where temperatures will remain more constant. Worms will freeze to death below 50 degrees F. When moving a bin indoors, however, consider that the worms will die if they get too hot as well — above 86 F. Ideally, worm bed temperature should be kept around 73 degrees F.

Another option to keep worms alive throughout the winter months is to insulate the bin. This can be done easily by using Styrofoam blocks and double-sided tape. The blocks should only be about an inch or two wide and can be cut to fit the bin. To begin winterizing the bin, remove the worms and their bedding into a clean bucket where the worms can hang out while you prepare their bin by following these easy steps:

1. Thoroughly clean the worm bin with warm water and let it air dry.

2. Once the bin is completely dry, attach the Styrofoam to the interior walls of the bin using the double-sided tape.

3. Add some straw to the bottom of the bin before returning the worms to their home.

It is important to monitor the temperature of the bin throughout the winter months to ensure the worms are not getting too cold, which brings up the question of how to tell if your worms are happy.

Checking the Worms: Are They Happy?

The worm bin should be monitored on a regular basis to ensure proper aeration, temperature, correct amount of grit provided for proper digestion, pH level, new bedding, and proper feeding. Now that you have done all of that, how do you know if your worms are happy?

The answer itself lies within two simple observations. 1. Your worms are growing, and the garbage they are being fed keeps disappearing. 2. After a month or so, you should start seeing miniature opaque eggs and little tiny thread-like baby worms. In other words, the worms will be eating well and making babies, two signs they are quite happy. The bigger question seems to be, how will you know if your worms are not happy?

FAMILY ACTIVITY:
Worm Tracker

Inquiry: How do we know if worms are happy?

Materials needed: For this activity, you will need a ruler; crayons, markers, or colored pencils; and your notebook or binder.

Project plan: Copy the following chart into your notebook or binder to track the needs and happiness of your worms. *The chart also is included in the Appendix, along with a checklist of worm needs to consider*

Monthly Sample Worm Tracker

Month: _____

	Week 1	Week 2	Week 3	Week 4
Temperature				
pH Level				
Bedding type				
Bedding changed				
Worms getting larger?				
Unwanted bugs				
Baby worms				

	Week 1	Week 2	Week 3	Week 4
Eggs or cocoons				
Notes:				

Questions to consider:

1. Are they getting everything they need to survive? Possible items to track include: temperature, correct amount of grit provided for proper digestion, pH level, new bedding and proper feeding.

2. After time, is the garbage, or worm food, disappearing?

3. Are the worms getting bigger?

4. Are there bugs in the bin?

5. Do you see little miniature eggs and baby worms?

What we learned: What have you learned from your observations? Are your worms "happy?" What do you think makes a worm happy?

Additional reading materials: Diary of a Worm by Doreen Cronin (Live oak Media, March 2004). The life of a worm as told through diary entries and humorous illustrations.

CHAPTER SIX

Common Concerns in the Worm Bin

".... its history affords a striking exemplification of the divine truth, that no creature has been formed without its special ends, and that the humblest are frequently selected to carry out the most gigantic natural operations."

JAMES SAMUELSON, AUTHOR OF *HUMBLE CREATURES: THE EARTHWORM AND THE COMMON HOUSEFLY, IN EIGHT LETTERS*

Even if you follow all the directions that come with your worm bin or the suggestions in this book, you still might encounter some common worm bin concerns. Growing and maintaining worms requires special attention and the ability to recognize problems that might arise, so they can be solved quickly. Because vermicomposting is one of the simplest forms of composting, the "problems" that creep up usually are remedied easily; there is no reason to panic when a problem arises.

Why Are My Worms Dying?

At some point, you might notice that the number of worms in your bin seems to be decreasing. You might have found some dead worms. The dead worms will decompose and be eaten by their friends. If this is the case, you will need to act quickly before all of your worms are gone. You will need to move your worms to a new bin, and fast. It might be a good idea to have an emergency bin ready in case of situations like this. If you do not have a backup bin, use anything you might have on hand. Worm emergency rooms can be set up in an old wooden box, a plastic bin, or a bucket. Make sure the container you are using is clean and chemical free. Fill the emergency bin with bedding and move the worms to the temporary bin. Then, check the vermicomposting system for the following possible problems:

Possible Problem	Solution
The bin is too wet and the worms are drowning.	Soak up as much water as you can. Replace the bedding with new dry bedding. Insert small rolls of newspaper throughout the bin to absorb water and help with proper airflow. Ensure the drainage holes are not blocked.
The bin is too dry and the worms cannot absorb the proper amount of oxygen to survive.	Add non-chlorinated water to the bin after making sure the drainage holes are open.

Possible Problem	Solution
There is not enough food for the worms. If the worms in a vermicomposting system run out of food, they will begin to eat their own castings. This is fatal to the worms.	Harvest the worms by removing the castings and start additional bins with the proper amount of food per pound of worm.
If the temperature is too cold, the worms will freeze to death.	Use a thermometer to determine the temperature in the worm bin. If it is too cold, move the vermicomposting system to a warmer location.
If the temperature is too hot, the worms will die.	If your bin is too hot, move the bin to a cooler location. Make sure the bin is kept out of direct sunlight.
The worms are getting too much direct light. Too much light can, in fact, kill the worms in a vermicomposting system.	Move the bin to a location that gets less light. Dark basements, out of direct sunlight, make the perfect location for a worm bin.
The pH level in the soil is incorrect. If the pH is too acid or alkaline, the worms can die.	Check the pH level in the bin and adjust accordingly. To lower the pH, add peat moss or coffee grounds. To raise the pH, add lime or hardwood ash.
The water that has been added to the vermicomposting system contains chlorine. The chlorinated water some communities have is harmful to the worm bin.	Ensure any water you add to your vermicomposting system is non-chlorinated. If you are on a public water supply, your water is most likely chlorinated. Some well-water systems also use chlorine. If you are unsure, use bottled spring water.

If none of the above problems seem to be an issue, try starting over. Throw away the old bedding and food. Wash the bin out with clean water, add new bedding, new food, and your worms. Closely monitor the bin to ensure that nothing changes, and act quickly if you find something off, such as the pH level, moisture level, or temperature.

Why Does the Bin Smell Foul?

Odors from the worm bin can be caused by several factors that might include overfilling it, a lack of air, too much moisture, too much acidity, smelly foods, or the wrong foods.

Odor-causing problem	Solution
Too much food waste: It is possible that you are feeding your worms too much food. If this is the case, the excess food that is not consumed in a timely manner will begin to rot and cause strong odors.	To solve the problem, break up any larger clumps of food in the bin and refrain from adding additional food until the problem is cleared up. You will need to give your worms some time to break down the food in the bin.
Lack of proper airflow: If your worm bin is not getting enough air, anaerobic bacteria will grow in the absence of oxygen and make your bin smell.	To create better airflow in the worm bin, gently stir up the entire bin to get more oxygen flowing. Repeat the gentle stirring for several days. Mixing in some additional worm bedding also can help create a better airflow. Ensure none of the air holes are blocked in the bin, as this will limit oxygen flow as well.

Odor-causing problem	Solution
Too much moisture: If your bin is too wet, the oxygen level in the bin will be limited and cause a bad smell.	The first step is to check the drainage holes to see if they are blocked. Blocked drainage will cause moisture levels to raise and air flow to cease. You also might be adding too much wet food to the bin, which would also cause the moisture level to rise. To prevent this, each time you add food to the bin, add a layer of bedding to help absorb the excess moisture.
Too acidic: If your pH levels are too acidic, below 6.0, this also will cause the bin to stink.	To balance the pH level, add broken up eggshells a couple of times a month. Rock dust also can be used sparingly to lower pH and provide grit for the worms.
High odor foods: Some foods, such as broccoli, just smell.	To limit the odor in the worm bin, avoid using foods that naturally have a pungent odor. Food such as broccoli also can be added one at a time to avoid a strong buildup of one food smell.
Improper food choice: Some foods are not intended to go in the worm compost bin and, as a result, will create strong odors as they decay.	As mentioned earlier, foods like meat, dairy, and oils should not go into a home vermicomposting system. These foods go rancid as they decompose and will cause lots of odor.

Why Are the Worms Not Eating?

Again, if the conditions in the vermicomposting system are not "just right," the worms will not function properly. If the amount of waste, or food, you add to the worm bin does not appear to be changing, consider the following:

1. Check the conditions of the bin. Go through the list of requirements specific to your worm type and ensure their unique requirements are being met. Check the temperature, moisture levels, and pH.

2. Is the bin new? Occasionally, when a new vermicomposting system is set up, the worms might be shocked and are slow to start eating. Worms need to get acclimated to their new home. If they are not eating the food right away, try waiting a few days and avoid adding more food until they are done with what they have in the bin.

Why Are My Worms Leaving and How Do I Keep Them In?

Worms are picky little creatures, which means if you do not provide them with an environment they like, they will leave you. Worms leave the bin in search of their preferred environment if it is not provided for them. Unfortunately, if you try blocking off the worms with a barrier, you run the danger of cutting off their oxygen supply and causing more harm than good. Some species of worms are choosier than others. Here are some tips if your worms leave the bin.

1. Know what type of worms you have. If you know the type of worm living in your vermicomposting system, you will be better able to provide for its specific needs. Always go by the scientific names for the worms, as many breeds often are called by the same name. Look up and abide by the specific requirements for moisture levels, acidity, and temperature. Knowing your worms' preferred diet also will help.

2. Because worms do not like sunlight, a light can be used to deter them from escaping the bin. Often, when the worms arrive or are sorted, they become stressed out and leave the bin in their harried state. Check first to make sure the conditions are right for your worms in their home. If they are still leaving, try leaving a bright light over the bin to encourage them to move into their bedding and get used to their new home.

Are My Worms Healthy?

Worms are not like the average household pet that requires regular visits to the vet and vaccines to keep healthy. Without calling in a worm expert, how will you know if the worms in your vermicomposting system are actually in good health? Not to mention the fact that your vet will probably not make a house visit to check on worms. An easy way to help monitor your worm bin is by keeping a chart when you check on the worms. *See the Appendix for a sample chart.*

Some tips to monitor the health of your worms include:

1. *Odor level:* If the worms in your vermicomposting system begin to smell, it is an indication of a larger problem that needs to be looked into. The bin should not have a foul smell.

2. *Eating habits:* There might be a problem if you notice that your worms have changed their eating habits. Are they eating less than they used to? Are they consuming more? If there is a noticeable difference in the worms' eating habits, check the conditions in the bin to ensure they meet your breed's requirements.

3. *Light them up:* Worms, when exposed to light, should quickly try to bury themselves. If they do not do this, they may be sick. Open the bin and shine a flashlight in. If the worms move quickly to hide, they are healthy. If they do not move or seem sluggish, something could be wrong. Double-check all the conditions in the bin to ensure proper requirements.

4. *Know your worms:* Any good pet owner or farmer will tell you, it is important to get to know your worms and their regular habits. By observing the worms when they are healthy, worm owners will be able to pick out unhealthy worms when they fall sick.

5. *Check their slime level:* Every worm has slime, or thin mucus, on its body. If the worms seem dry, this could be a sign of a larger problem. If the worms seem too dry, check all the conditions in the bin to make sure there is proper moisture, aeration, temperature, and pH levels.

Should Mushrooms Be Growing in My Bin?

Dark, damp conditions often lend themselves to the growth of mushrooms. Home vermicomposting systems are no exception and can sometimes breed mushrooms. This is nothing to be concerned about. Mushrooms are an indicator that fungi are present. Fungi are a natural part of the decomposition process and will not do any harm in the worm bin. The appearance of mushrooms is a good indicator that the temperature in your bin is somewhere between 70 and 75 degrees, which is perfect for red worms. Just pull the mushrooms out of the bin and throw them away. Do not eat these mushrooms, and wash your hands afterward.

Is Mold a Sign Something Is Wrong?

Another organism in the decomposition process is mold. It is not always visible, however, and those new to vermicomposting might become concerned when they discover it. Mold usually becomes visible when the food is not buried enough. The appearance of mold is not an issue unless you are allergic to it. If you are allergic to molds, you might want to keep your bin outdoors and make sure you bury the worm food deeply. Mold is not harmful to worms.

What Do I Do if I Have Too Many Worms?

If you have made the worms happy, another problem that may inadvertently crop up is overcrowding in the bin and an excess of worms. When conditions are favorable (i.e. proper temperature, moisture, and food), red worms will mature and begin mating at eight weeks old. Two to three cocoons per week can result per worm. From these cocoons, two to five baby worms will hatch in about three weeks' gestation period. Let us say, for example, one worm produces two cocoons per week with five baby worms per cocoon. That would be five offspring per week per worm. Eight weeks from being born, that offspring can start producing as well. And, so, it continues with each additional generation.

Fun Fact: In the "wild," worms usually live only about one year. In a worm bin with the proper care, worms can live up to about four years. Imagine how many worms one worm and its offspring can reproduce in four years.

Without getting too detailed into the reproductive numbers, in about a 26-week period, the original two worms (first generation), their offspring (second generation), and the next set of offspring (third generation) will have totaled about 8,455 worms. Now, what to do with all those worms?

Some ideas include:

1. Give them away. Some people who might be interested in worms include garden centers, horse ranches, dairies (to vermicompost manure), fishermen, bait shops, bird owners, farms with game birds, pet stores (for food), scientific researchers (for experiments), commercial worm growers, schools, home-schooling families, scouts, or even waste treatment plants.

2. Create an additional worm bin to compost even more household waste.

3. Sell the extra worms by placing ads on Craigslist or in farming magazines.

4. Add the worms to your outdoor garden to work their magic there. Be aware, however, that some varieties of worms will not survive in certain climates.

5. If you are in a warmer climate, try making an outdoor vermicomposting bed, as they require a larger amount of worms to be productive.

6. Use them to go fishing, or feed them to household animals, such as chickens, fish, turtles, frogs, or lizards.

7. Donate a vermicomposting bin complete with worms to a community garden, church, school, or family member.

8. Profit from your good fortune and start a worm-farming business to sell worms to other would-be worm farmers. *Tips for making a business out of your worms is discussed in Chapter 10.*

CHAPTER SEVEN

Other Critters in the Bin

"A man may fish with the worm that hath eat of a king, and eat of the fish that hath fed of that worm."

**WILLIAM SHAKESPEARE ON THE
EARTHWORM'S TRANSFORMATIVE POWER**

In addition to your worms, other creatures in the form of bugs and other organisms will make their way into the home vermicomposting system. Some of these will be beneficial, and others will not. The "good" creatures are organisms that help in the decomposition process and are necessary to ensure a healthy worm bin. These include the first-level, second-level, and third-level consumers.

First, Second, and Third Level Consumers

To recap, first-level consumers are the organisms that consume waste directly. First-level consumers include molds, bacteria, earthworms, beetle mites, sowbugs, and enchytraeids. Flies also are considered first-level consumers, as they also consume waste directly. Second-level consumers in a compost pile eat first-level consumers as well as the waste of the first-level consumers. These little guys include springtails, bacteria (yes, again), mold mites, feather-winged beetles, and actinomycetes. Protozoa, when eating bacteria, also function as a second-level consumer.

An organism's function within the vermicompost pile can change depending upon its food source at the time. For example, an earthworm eating a leaf is a first-level consumer. When the same worm consumes the bacteria that decayed a fruit peel, it is acting as a second-level consumer.

Third-level consumers are called the "flesh-eating," or predatory, critters in the worm bin. These guys eat both the first- and second-level consumers and include creatures like centipedes, ants, predatory mites, and rove beetles.

CASE STUDY: A KNOWLEDGEABLE STUDENT

Samantha Vigue
Jr. high school student/home gardener
Durham, Connecticut
Level of expertise: I think I've got the hang of it. (Knowledgeable)

Samantha Vigue is an articulate junior high school student who, along with selling crafts at the local farmers markets with her grandmother and uncle, is interested in gardening and vermicomposting. In addition to having a household vermicomposting system, Vigue also participates in a vermicomposting project at school. At home, Vigue and her family have a six-layer bin. At school, they have a slightly smaller four-layer bin.

A vermicomposter for nearly three years, Vigue is an expert at what can "go wrong" in the worm bin. Fruit flies, for example, have been a big concern with her home vermicomposting system. Because the worm food is gathered in the kitchen, she discovered that by emptying the worm food more frequently into the bin, it kept the fruit flies out of the kitchen. "We also found some interesting fruit fly traps that seemed to work well."

In the basement, where the worm bin is located, Vigue tried the fruit fly traps with little success. Instead, she covered the worm bin with a large piece of cloth with fine holes to restrict the flies from getting into the bin. She also discovered that if she carried the bin outside whenever possible to maintain it, it helped keep the fly population down as well. Her big fruit fly deterrent discovery, however, was to place a dry layer of crumpled paper in between the active food areas. By doing this, "The fly populations have greatly reduced."

In addition to knowing what does not belong in the bin, Vigue is also knowledgeable about what does belong. "If you see little white things in your worm bin, do not panic," she says, "These mites eat the food like the worms but do not hurt the worms."

Vigue and her family use worm tea in the garden "like we are watering the plants" and says that "vermicomposting has greatly reduced our garbage output."

Beneficial, Harmful, or Just a Pest?

With all of these creatures roaming around the worm bin, which ones are beneficial, which harmful, and which are just a nuisance? Ants, as an example, most likely will not do any damage in the bin. Streams of ants, however, crossing the floor into the bin will be quite a nuisance as they search for the food you have been hiding there. Centipedes, on the other hand, are fast-moving predatory creatures looking to make a meal out of the worms living in the bin. These should be destroyed, or they will feast on your worm friends.

The following is a chart to help identify visitors in the bin, some information on them, and how to prevent them, if needed:

Bin Visitor	Details	Prevention Tips
Ants	Ants find their way into the worm bin because they are looking for food. Ants will not actually harm the worms, but they can be nuisances if they come unwelcome into your home.	To eradicate ants from the worm bin, follow their trail to find out how they are getting into the bin. Prevention is key. Plug any holes or cracks they might be coming in through. Use a natural "barrier" ants will not cross, such as lemon juice, mentholated rubs, talcum powder, cayenne pepper, or most strong-scented cleaners. To get rid of the ants you see, spray window cleaner or lemon extract on a paper towel, and wipe down the worm bin. Use the same substance to wipe the floor along the trail they used to enter the bin.
Centipedes	Centipedes are quick moving and are looking to eat the worms in your bin. They are arthropods and live in humus and soil. They can range from one inch to one foot, are flat, and come in various colors.	Centipedes discovered in the worm bin need to be destroyed immediately or they will kill the worms. You will need to squish them with your garden shovel or trowel. Their sting is painful to humans.
Enchytraeid worms	Enchytraeid are small white worms that are actually relatives of the red worm. Like earthworms, they eat decomposing plant matter and burrow through the soil.	Do not be concerned if these pop up in your bin.

Bin Visitor	Details	Prevention Tips
Flies	There are thousands of species of flies and any number of them might enjoy hovering around your vermicomposting system.	To prevent flies, keep a screen cover on your food wastes before putting the food in the worm bin so the flies cannot lay eggs in it. Bury all the food, do not overfeed the worms, use a varied diet for the worms, and place newspaper or cloth over the bin to prevent flies.
Grubs	Grubs look like white naked shrimp and are not bad visitors to the worm bin.

Grubs are actually the infant form of beetles. They are c-shaped and range in size up to two inches. Grubs help break down larger pieces of material into smaller ones that can be eaten by worms and other smaller organisms. | They are not troublesome in a worm bin, but they can be removed by handpicking. |
| Millipedes | Millipedes are wormlike creatures that are big, fat, round, and segmented. They have lots of legs and range in size from a half inch to two inches. Millipedes also break down larger materials into smaller pieces. | They are harmless, but they can be removed by handpicking. |

Bin Visitor	Details	Prevention Tips
Mites	Mites look like tiny dots moving quickly. They are often discovered on the worm bedding. They are only about $1/50$th of an inch. In well-maintained vermicomposting systems, mite numbers are kept in control. The number of mites, however, can build up if the conditions are wet and acidic. If the mite population is too high, the worms will not come to the surface to feed.	To prevent mites, keep the pH at a proper level of 7. Keep the bin from getting too wet, and do not overfeed the worms. To get a large mite population under control, try the following: Expose the bin to sunlight for several hours, reduce the amount of food and water in the bin, place moist paper towels on top of the bin to collect the mites, and change the bedding.
Slugs	Slug often make their way into the worm bin to seek shelter, shade, and food.	If slugs become a problem in your vermicomposting system, handpick them out and drown them in a bucket of soapy water. Also, make sure all food is properly buried. You also can deter slugs by sprinkling diatomaceous earth around the legs of your worm bin.
Springtails	Springtails look like white dots and are only one to three millimeters long. Springtails are named for their jumping abilities and are usually found living in the soil under leaf litter and in decaying wood. Springtails are a key player in the production of humus and beneficial to the worm bin.	Springtails are helpful to the vermicomposting process and do not need to be removed.

Grub

With all of these organisms living in the worm bin, it is only natural to wonder if there might be disease organisms living or growing in the vermicomposting system. For example, could you, your pets, or other members of your household catch a germ, virus, or other disease from your worm bin? In general, the answer would be no. A home vermicomposting system, however, does not generate enough heat to kill harmful pathogens effectively. With this in mind, remember to not use cat, dog, or human waste in the worm bin. Although some research suggests using worms in sewer sludge might reduce the number of pathogens, research is inconclusive and ongoing. If you are allergic or overly sensitive to mold spores, having a worm bin inside might not be for you, as molds develop naturally in a vermicomposting system as part of the natural process.

Overall, there are plenty of critters in the worm bin alongside the actual worms. In reality, these party crashers are a necessary part of a vermicomposting system. The system, as a whole, would not work without the other organisms playing their roles. Each species provides a food source for another, helps clean up debris, and controls one another's population. Organic materials, such as vermicompost, are likely to contain great numbers of soil organisms. So, in the end, who are we to say who does or does not belong in there?

A better question might be, "How we can harvest the worms and use the vermicastings?"

FAMILY ACTIVITY:
It's a Bug Life

Inquiry: What kind of bugs move into the worm bin?

Materials needed: Modeling clay, reference book on bugs (refer to the bugs listed in this chapter), pencils, and your notebook or binder.

Project plan: Referring to a bug reference book, create the different bugs that are found in the worm bin (ants, centipedes, flies, grubs, and worms) with the modeling clay.

Questions to consider:

1. Using the chart in this chapter, which ones are helpful in the worm bin?

2. Which bugs are not useful in the bin?

3. What are the characteristics of each bug you made?

4. Do the bugs help each other out? In what ways?

What we learned: Write down what you learned about the various bugs that cohabit the bin.

Additional reading materials: *Simon & Schuster Children's Guide to Insects and Spiders* by Jinny Johnson (Simon & Schuster Books For Young Readers, May 1997).

CHAPTER EIGHT

Harvesting

> *"I think we consider too much the good luck of the early bird and not enough the bad luck of the early worm."*
>
> **FRANKLIN D. ROOSEVELT**

The bins have been set up, the worms are happy, the rhythm of collecting waste and feeding the worms has been established, and you have made friends with the worms and are able to know when the conditions in the bin might need to be adjusted. Now what? The time has come to harvest and sort to be able to use the fruits of your labor, not to mention those hardworking worms. Questions that you might already have include: When will the compost be ready? How will I know when the compost is ready? Can I harvest vermicompost and vermicastings separately? How do I harvest? How should compost be stored? *All of these questions, and more, will be covered in this chapter.*

When Will My Compost Be Ready?

Vermicastings

The easiest way to tell when the vermicompost is ready is when you look in the bin and all or most of the original bedding is gone. The original bedding will have been "changed" into a dark brown to black, earthy-looking vermicompost. Vermicompost is a mixture of decomposed organic matter and vermicastings, or worm excrement. The process takes anywhere from a few weeks to six months, based on the size of the bin and the number of worms. The longer you let the worms work, the finer and richer the vermicompost will be and eventually turn to vermicastings only. The downside, however, is that the longer the worms work, the fewer worms you will have in the bin, as they will die off due to living in their own excrement for longer periods. My recommendation would be to harvest somewhere in the middle at about the three-month mark to find a happy balance between the two. If you choose to wait longer until the product has turned into vermicastings only, you can still follow the same harvesting methods.

How to Harvest the Vermicompost

You can harvest from the vermicomposting system a few different ways. Something to consider is whether you are only harvesting the compost/castings or if you would also like to harvest some of the worms at the same time. This decision will affect the process through which you harvest.

Fun Fact: Worm castings are good at absorbing moisture, are odorless, and have the ability to reduce unpleasant smells. Because of this, worm castings make a great cat litter.

For example, if you only want to harvest only the vermicompost without the worms, try this method:

1. Stop feeding the worms until all the food in the bin has been consumed.

2. Once all the food has been consumed, move all of the bedding material (including the worms) over to one side of the bin, leaving plenty of room to add new bedding on the other side.

3. Place new bedding on the cleared side, and add in some food.

4. Leave the worms alone for a couple of days.

5. After a few days, the worms will have migrated from the old bedding over to the new bedding in search of food.

6. The old bedding, which should be mostly vermicompost/castings at this point, will still contain some worms along with cocoons. Worm cocoons are about the size of a sesame seed and are extremely difficult and time consuming to remove from the vermicompost.

7. At this point, there are two options. You can take the old bedding (vermicompost) complete with the slow worms and cocoons to start a new worm bin. Or, you can use the vermicompost directly in the garden, in houseplants, or for sale.

A note about worm eggs:

Worm eggs (or cocoons), often referred to as worm capsules, are very tiny, about the size of a sesame seed. As such, they will fit through a ¼-inch screen. During the process of sorting vermicompost from the worms, it would be very time consuming to try to sort the worm capsules from the vermicompost, nearly impossible in some cases. If the presence of worm capsules in the compost bothers you, let the compost sit for a couple of months. By that time, the eggs will have hatched and the screening method can be used to separate the baby worms from the vermicastings. The babies can then be used to start a new bin or added to the existing bin.

On gloves: It is recommended to use gloves when handling vermicompost, the worms, or the worm capsules. Natural skin oils are thought to break the surface of the worm eggs. In addition, various forms of mold in the bin might cause allergic reactions in some people.

There are a variety of other harvest sorting methods for removing the vermicompost/castings, including sorting directly in the bin, screening, moving, bag, water, light, death, and direct to garden. Each method has its own pros and cons.

Bag method

The bag method involves luring the worms into a netted bag with sweet treats to separate the worms from the vermicompost. This method involves patience, is simple, and requires little physical work. For this harvesting technique, you will need:

- A mesh onion bag or nylon delicates laundry bag with openings large enough for the worms to crawl through

- Two to three clean, empty buckets to gather the finished vermicompost and worms

- Sweet treats for the worms, such as kiwis, melons, or apples

- Large plastic sheet or garbage bag

Process:

1. Do not feed the worms for about ten days, as you want them to be hungry.

2. Fill the bag with some of the worms' favorite foods. Sweet treats such as apple pieces, melon peels, and kiwis are ideal.

3. Bury the filled bag in the same location you normally bury the food.

4. Leave it there for one to three days.

5. At this point, the worms should have migrated into the bag. If they have not, leave the bag another day or so until they do so.

6. Lay down the plastic sheet or garbage bag on your work area.

7. Place the empty buckets on the plastic along with your worm bin.

8. Move the bag with the worms in it to one of the empty buckets, and gently set it down. Cover the bucket lightly to ensure airflow still gets to the worms.

9. Beginning in the opposite corner of where the worms were last fed, pull out the finished compost by hand and place in the other empty bucket. There should be very few worms. If you do come across some stragglers, gently add them to the other bucket containing the worms in the bag.

10. As you get closer to the location where the bag with the food was buried, you may come across more and more worms.

11. Once all the worms and compost have been sorted, build a new bed in the bin for the worms.

12. Return the bag of worms and any stragglers to the bin, leaving them in the bag.

13. After about a week, feed the worms in the opposite corner from where you placed them back in the bin in the bag.

14. In a matter of a few days, the worms will have migrated to the next food corner, and you should be able to lift the bag up and shake it free of any vermicompost.

This is a great method to help you keep track of the number of worms that you currently have in your bin because you can see the total amount as they gather in the bag. This would be a great time to practice a little population control. You either could start another bin or give away or sell the extra worms.

Death and modified death technique

This method is best for people who do not mind buying new worms on a regular basis. It is also good for people who do not want to or who do not have the time to sort and separate. The death technique allows all of the worms to die in the bin, while the modified death method allows some of the worms to live.

The steps to this death technique include:

1. Set up the worm bin, and feed the worms on a regular basis as discussed in earlier chapters.

2. Continue to feed the worms for two to four months.

3. Next, stop feeding the worms completely, leaving them to continue to eat through the compost.

4. In about another three to four months, all of the worms will be dead and decomposed with only vermicastings remaining.

5. Remove the vermicastings for use as compost.

6. Start the bin over with fresh bedding and brand new worms.

The disadvantage to this method is that you will have to find an alternate means of disposing of your compost during this time.

Vermicastings versus vermicompost

The terms vermicastings and vermicompost are used interchangeably, but is there a difference between the two? Vermicast is used to refer to the material that has been worked and reworked until it has very little decomposing organic material left in it. It has a smoother texture than vermicompost but does not necessarily have any more nutrients than vermicompost. Vermicompost, on the other hand, is the stage before it gets to vermicastings. It is slightly chunkier with more organic materials that have not been fully decomposed. In the case of the above harvesting technique, you will be harvesting vermicastings due to not feeding the worms.

The modified death technique, on the other hand, allows some of the worms to live. This method does, however, require the use of two worm bins. To use this method:

1. Start one worm bin as discussed earlier in the book.

2. When it is time to harvest, place some of the worms favorite sweet treats such as cantaloupe, kiwi, or apples on top of the bin to draw as many worms as possible to the top.

3. Prepare a second bin with bedding.

4. After a day or two, dig down and transfer the worms that came to the top to get the food into the second bin.

5. Continue to feed the worms in the second bin, but not those left in the first bin.

In this technique, the worms left in the first bin will continue to turn the vermicompost into vermicastings, creating a smooth product until they all eventually die. The benefit to this method is that while you have a working bin with worms that continue to eat your weekly waste, you will have another crew creating a rich well-processed product.

Direct to garden

This method is probably the simplest method out there. When you are ready to harvest the bin, remove about one-half of its contents, and take it directly to the garden. Add the worms and the vermicompost directly into the garden by gently working it into the top layers of the soil. Ensure the worms have enough decaying matter to survive in the garden on their own by placing a few dead leaves on top.

Add additional bedding to the half left empty in the worm bin and begin the vermicomposting process all over again.

Light method

Because worms are photophobic (they shun the light), light can be used to help sort the worms from the vermicompost for an easy collection method. For this technique, you will need:

- Large piece of plastic sheeting or a large trash bag to dump the contents of the worm bin onto
- A lighting source: an overhead light if you are working indoors or the sun if outdoors

- Plastic pan or other container for the worms
- Heavy plastic bag or metal or plastic container for the vermicompost
- New bedding

Instructions:

1. Spread the plastic sheet or garbage bag on the ground or work area.

2. Gently dump the bin and all of its contents onto the plastic.

3. Using your hands, make about nine pyramid-shaped piles.

4. The worms should begin to move toward the bottom of the piles to hide from the light.

5. At this point, you can start picking up worms as you see them and moving them to the container you have designated to hold the worms while you work.

6. After about five to ten minutes, all the worms should have moved into the bottoms and centers of the pyramid piles.

7. Gently remove the outer surface of each pile. The worms will push even closer together to hide themselves from being exposed to the light.

8. Gently remove a little more dirt from each pile. Continue the process.

9. Eventually, all the worms will collect in a mass in the bottom of each pile.

10. Gently scoop up the piles of worms and add them to the collecting bin.

11. Replace the bedding in the worm bin and return the worms you have collected.

12. The vermicompost will be left on the plastic sheeting and can be used directly in the garden.

Moving method

The moving method is ideal for larger bins that are difficult to move due to their size and weight. When the bin is ready to be harvested, follow these simple steps:

1. Gently push the contents of the vermicomposting bin over to one side of the container.

2. Add new bedding to the empty side of the bin.

3. Place food on the new side only.

4. After several days, the worms will move over to the "new" side for food and clean bedding.

5. Once the worms have moved over to the new side, harvest the "old" side.

6. Add new bedding to the "old" side and repeat the process.

Screening method

This sorting technique involves using a screen to sift through the worms and separate them from the vermicompost/vermicastings. There are two methods to this technique: dumping the worms onto a screen or using a screen directly in the bin. To use the first method, you will need:

• A large plastic sheet or garbage bag

• A framed screen with a mesh about ¼ or 3⁄16 of an inch

Follow these steps:

1. Place the plastic sheeting on the ground of your workspace.

2. Place the screen on top of the plastic.

3. Dump the contents of the worm bin onto the screen.

4. Gently lift the screen. The vermicompost will drop through, leaving behind the worms and larger particles of matter and food.

5. Return the worms to the vermicomposting bin, complete with new bedding.

6. Gather up the vermicompost from the plastic to use in the garden.

The downside of this technique is that it tends to stress the worms, and they may take a while to get back into the swing of things again once you return them to their home.

To use a screen-sorting method within the worm bin, place a piece of ³⁄₁₆-inch flexible screen on top of the worm bin when you are getting ready to harvest. Use a large enough piece of screen so the edges will go up the sides of the bin to make lifting it out of the bin easier. Add new bedding to the bin directly on top of the screen. Add food to the new bedding. The worms will move upward through the screening to reach the new food and bedding.

Once the worms have migrated, lift the screen complete with bedding and worms out of the top of the bin and place it on a plastic sheet or garbage bag. Remove the vermicompost/vermicastings from the worm bin and replace the contents from on top of the screen back into the bin. Repeat the process again in another two to three months when the vermicompost is ready to harvest again.

Sorting directly in the bin

This technique is the least disruptive to the worms, but it does require you to get your hands dirty and is ideal for smaller bins. It also allows gives you control over how much or little you remove at one time. To use this process, follow these simple steps:

1. Carefully separate the uneaten food and worms from the vermicompost/vermicastings.

2. Use a soft-bristled paintbrush to push the vermicompost/vermicastings over to one side.

3. Scoop the compost out of the bin and place it in a plastic or metal bucket or container. A plastic trash bag will work as well.

4. In a few minutes, the worms will begin moving deeper into the bin.

5. Start the process over until you have collected as much vermicompost as you need.

6. Toward the end, there will be more worms left in the bin than vermicompost. This is a good time to remove any extra worms for other uses.

7. Once you are done, add new bedding, and continue to feed the worms as discussed in earlier chapters.

Water method

Worm castings, when used in their liquid form, are an incredibly nutrient-rich and simple way to add compost to the garden. One way in which to do this is to dissolve the worm castings in water. To do this, spray the worm bin with water and collect the water that pools in the bottom of the bin. Remember not to waterlog your worms for too long, as this will kill them. Add new, dry bedding to the bin as soon as possible. Some home vermicomposting systems come complete with a bottom tray that collects water and has a spigot for easy gathering of the water.

Method	Pros	Cons
Bag	• Lets the worms do the work of separating • Clean and easy	• Requires patience
Death	• Hands-off • Simple	• Need to purchase new worms and start the process of vermicomposting over again
Direct to Garden	• Extremely simple • No sorting involved • Not messy	• Need to ensure worms have enough food in their new location
Light	• Easy • Lets the worms sort themselves	• Need to get hands dirty
Moving	• Good for large systems • Worms naturally sort themselves	• Requires attention and getting hands dirty
Screening	• Cleanly separates worms from vermicompost	• Stressful to the worms
Sorting Directly in the Bin	• Do not need to remove contents of bin to sort	• Need to get hands dirty
Water	• Produces a highly concentrated liquid compost	• Could potentially drown and kill worms if not careful

How to Store Vermicompost

Now that you have all of this wonderful compost, how should it be stored? Ideally, vermicomposting should be used directly in the garden or near plants when it is harvested. *How to use the vermicompost in the garden will be discussed in the next chapter.* There may be some cases, however, in which there is too much vermicompost, or you want to store it to give it away or sell.

Good compost, such as what the worms have manufactured in the vermicomposting system, will be filled with aerobic organisms. This means that oxygen is vital to their survival, and the vermicompost should not be stored in a completely sealed bag or container. If vermicompost were to be stored in such a manner, the oxygen will be consumed very quickly. What this means is that the conditions would become anaerobic. Anaerobic conditions will kill off the beneficial aerobic organisms in the vermicompost. Not to mention, anaerobic conditions will lead to the production of compounds that are harmful to the plants instead of beneficial.

Ideally, vermicompost should be stored in a dry, cool location that provides adequate airflow without letting it dry completely out, while keeping it slightly moist. On the other hand, vermicompost should not be stored too wet either. To accomplish this, follow these tips:

- If the compost is too wet when you harvest it, spread the compost out on a newspaper and let it dry out for a while.
- The compost should be a nice crumbly texture and should not feel damp or wet when you touch it.

- Plastic bags can be used to store vermicompost, but many holes will need to be poked in the bag. The challenge will be making the holes small enough, so the vermicompost does not fall out.

- Any type of container you use to store the vermicompost should allow for lots of air exchange. A Rubbermaid container, for example, can be used if it has some holes for ventilation and a loose-fitting cover.

- Vermicompost should not be stored outside where it is exposed to the elements. Rain will wash not only the compost away but also will wash away any nutrients in it.

- The sun can dry out the vermicompost as well.

How to Store Vermicastings

Is storing vermicasting the same as vermicompost? Ideally, vermicastings, like their compost counterpart, should be used directly in the garden or in plants when it is harvested. *How to use the vermicastings in the garden will be discussed in the next chapter.* However, pure castings, unlike vermicompost, can be stored in airtight containers without the need to provide for airflow. A zippered plastic bag or covered plastic container are ideal for storing castings.

Family Activity: Photophobic Worms

Inquiry: How do worms react when exposed to light?

Materials needed: For this project, you will need a pencil for notes, your notebook or binder, a handful of worms, wet paper towels, some water, an aluminum pie pan, a small flashlight, black construction paper, and a bucket of dirt to keep the worms in.

Project plan:

1. Add wet paper towels to the bottom of the aluminum pan.

2. Add some dirt from the bucket to the bottom of the pan (about an inch or two deep) and moisten with some water. (The wet towels and the water are to keep the worms moist so they do not dry out.)

3. Add the worms to the top of the soil. Gently shine the flashlight on them, being careful to not get too close and burn them.

4. Record their behavior.

5. Cover the pan completely with the black paper, and wait five minutes.

6. Remove the cover.

7. Record what happens.

Questions to consider:

1. What did the worms do when you shined the light on them?

2. Did they come closer to the surface again after you covered them with paper?

What we learned: Worms are photophobic, which means they shun the light.

Additional reading materials: *A Project Guide to Sponges, Worms, and Mollusks* (Life Science Projects for Kids) by Colleen Kessler (Mitchell Lane Publishers, October 2010). This book is a guide to hands-on activities, projects, and experiments to learn about sponges, worms, and mollusks.

CHAPTER NINE

Using Worm Compost and Castings

> *"We are all worms. But I believe that I am a glow-worm."*
> **WINSTON CHURCHILL**

Vermicompost, the rich mixture of organic materials, is the main reason gardeners keep a worm bin. To review, vermicompost is the dark mixture that includes worm castings, bedding materials, organic matter, living earthworms, cocoons, and other various organisms. Vermicastings, on the other hand, are the deposits that once moved through the worm and its digestive tract. As discussed in the previous chapter, the worms need to work "longer" to produce a viable amount of castings. Worm castings are a biologically active material that contains thousands of bacteria at work.

 **Fun Fact:** Regular compost can take up to 240 days for a gardener to make. Worms, on the other hand, can make vermicompost, in just 30 days.

Benefits of Vermicompost

An important benefit of vermicompost is the creation of humus. As you might recall from an earlier chapter, humus is a complex and nutrient-rich material that is created during the breakdown of organic matter. Humus includes things such as iron, calcium, potassium, phosphorus, and sulfur. These nutrients are important to plant health and growth as well as in aiding in the control of harmful fungi and bacteria.

Other benefits of compost include:

- An increased level of microbial activity in the soil
- Improved water retention in the soil
- Extremely high nutrient levels and the availability of the nutrients to the soil itself
- Less compacted soils, which lead to better aeration
- A decrease in plant and soil disease and pests

Using Vermicompost

There is a multitude of ways to use worms and worm products in the garden. In general, worms can be added directly to the soil where they can do their work "on location," so to speak; their castings can be used as a compost to improve the soil, and water runoff from the worm bin can be used as a fertilizer in the garden and for houseplants.

Seedbeds

Unlike commercial fertilizers, vermicompost will not "burn" your plants. Because of the amount of vermicompost a home composting system produces, it makes sense to use it where it will do the most good. Seedbeds, for example, are the perfect place to reap the benefits of vermicompost. Vermicompost can be added directly to the seedbeds by sprinkling it into the seed row trench along with the seeds. Cover loosely with soil. This method provides the seeds with a burst of rich nutrients as they germinate and throughout the early stages of growth.

Transplants

When transplanting garden plants from veggies to perennials, vermicompost can be used to help make the transition easier on the plant. Seedlings can be moved from growing trays to the garden and will thrive with the addition of a few sprinkles of vermicompost mixed into their new home. Likewise, when transplanting a plant from one pot to another, adding vermicompost will add much-needed nutrients as the plant settles into its new home.

Top dressing

A "top dressing" is the term used to describe adding compost, in this case vermicompost, to the base of a plant already established in the ground. This is an easy way to add nutrients without disturbing the plant's root system. Nutrients become available to the plant as water drips through the vermicompost and pushes it down through the soil. Vermicompost also can be sprinkled into the dirt of your houseplants.

Adding worms directly to the garden

Earthworms are in the business of making great soil, which is why they make excellent visitors to the garden. Earthworms generally inhabit in the top 12 to 18 inches of the soil. As discussed throughout the book, worms have many benefits for the soil. In some cases, earthworms already will be prevalent in your garden.

Using Vermicastings

Vermicastings are the finer result of the vermicomposting process. What makes the casting differ from the compost is that the castings look in appearance to be closer to rich, dark dirt. Castings do not have the "chunks" or pieces of worm bedding and food scraps that the compost usually contains. Vermicastings are like gold in the fertilizer world.

The nutrient content in vermicastings, which varies depending on the types of foods the worms are fed, is much higher than that of vermicompost. Castings do not contain the bacterially composted bedding and organic food that vermicompost does. Pure castings have a higher pH, and you will need to take care when adding castings to acid-loving plants, as they do not tolerate a high pH level.

Some gardeners prefer to mix castings directly into potting soil. This process provides necessary nutrients for plants while diluting the heavy salt content that castings sometimes can have. Because castings can have a high salt content, they should not be used as a sole potting medium and need to be mixed with another medium like potting soil. For example, pure castings can be added at a ratio of 5 percent castings to the potting soil. Adding this small amount of castings will increase  plant growth and strength due to the high nitrogen and carbolic acid levels present in the castings. Castings work as a type of hormone to promote better plant growth.

Experimenting with different ratios for different plants is a good idea when considering how to add vermicastings to your potting soil. A good experiment is to take three of the same plants and add a vermicastings/ potting soil ratio of 5 to 95 percent to the first plant. To the second plant, create a mix of 15 percent castings to 85 percent soil, and to the last plant, a mix of 25 percent castings to 75 percent soil. Do any of them seem to grow better than the other? If the plant in 5 percent castings does just as well as the one in 25 percent castings, use the mix of 5 percent, as it will save on castings use.

Castings can help both plants and animals develop a resistance to certain diseases. Chicks that eat castings as part of their diet became more resistant to salmonella infections. In other cases, when castings were applied to the soil around the base of certain trees, the trees became more resistant to root rot diseases.

In conclusion, castings can be used in many of the same ways as the compost. Castings are, however, more concentrated in strength and do not need to be used at full-force. Some things to keep in mind when using the castings only include:

- **As a top dressing fertilizer:** When applying castings as a top-dressing fertilizer, they can become very dry and form a crust on the soil surface. This crust will limit water penetration. To avoid the formation of a crust, castings will need to be well watered. In addition to adding castings as a top-dressing fertilizer to the outdoor plants, they also can be sprinkled into the tops of houseplant pots and watered well.

- **As a mulch:** Use castings as a mulch, about two inches thick, around trees and other plants, but be careful not to put the castings too close to the stem or trunk. Remember to keep watered well.

- **To help transplants settle in:** Add a small amount of castings to the transplant hole before adding the plant that is being moved. Add the plant and water well to dilute the castings. This method also can be used for houseplants. Instead of using castings directly, mix equal parts of potting soil and castings when moving houseplants from a smaller pot to a larger one and water well. This method will help the plant settle into its new home with much-needed nutrients for survival.

- **To add to lawns and garden soil:** Castings can be used as a soil amendment to both lawns and large garden beds by sprinkling over the surface area about ¼-inch thick.

Making Worm Tea

Worm tea is simple to make and highly beneficial in the garden. Worm tea offers a host of benefits to the garden including:

- Improving water retention

- Growing healthy plants that yield healthier blooms, fruits, and vegetables

- Acting as a natural bug repellent for garden pests as well as a fungicide

- Creating a healthier soil that helps promote plant growth

Worm tea is not the water runoff from the vermicomposting bin. That runoff is actually called leachate, and it contains undissolved solids and potential harmful bacteria. Worm tea, on the other hand, is worm castings that have been soaked in water and properly oxygenated.

The additional oxygen creates an increase in the good bacteria along with the added benefit of additional nutrients. These nutrients include nitrogen, phosphate, calcium, and magnesium.

To make worm tea, gather the following items:

- A 5-gallon bucket
- Non-chlorinated water
- Three to five handfuls of worm castings
- A muslin bag or pantyhose
- One tablespoon of molasses
- An air pump/bubbler like those used in small home aquariums

Directions:

1. Fill the bucket about three quarters of the way with non-chlorinated water.

2. Insert the pump/bubbler and allow it to run in the water for an hour or two.

3. Add the castings and molasses.

4. Allow the mixture to aerate with the filter going for 24 hours.

How to Use Worm Tea

Worm tea will not last indefinitely. In fact, it should be used as soon as possible to reap its benefits fully. If the worm tea smells, it has gone bad. Do not use it. The easiest way to use the worm tea is to put it in a spray bottle and spray it directly on the plants or even the lawn. It also can be used to directly water the plants. For example, you can add the worm tea directly to a watering can and water the plants as you normally would.

Family Activity: Cucumber in a Bottle

Inquiry: Will a cucumber grow in a bottle if the soil is nutrient-rich enough?

Materials needed: For this activity, you will need an outdoor garden plot, a cucumber seedling, a plastic 2-liter bottle, a pick, water, soil, vermicompost, a pencil, and your notebook or binder.

Project plan: To grow a cucumber in a bottle, do the following steps:

1. Work the vermicompost into the soil in an outdoor garden plot.

2. Dig a hole for the cucumber seedling.

3. Add a handful of vermicompost to the bottom of the hole.

4. Add the plant to the hole, cover with soil and water well.

5. While you are waiting for the cucumber plant to grow, poke holes all around the bottle.

6. When the plant starts to develop tiny cucumbers, gently place one through the opening of the bottle. Shade the bottle with the leaves of the cucumber plant so it does not get too hot.

7. Continue to water the plant, adding a small amount of vermicompost to the plant every other week or so.

8. Try the experiment with a cucumber plant without adding the vermicompost to compare results.

9. Draw a picture of the cucumber in the bottle in your journal.

Questions to consider:

1. Did the cucumber grow inside the bottle?

2. Do you think that adding the vermicompost made a difference in the plant's growth?

3. Did this project make gardening more fun for you?

4. How are you going to get the cucumber out to eat it?

What we learned: Write down your thoughts on why adding vermicompost might have helped the cucumber plant grow.

Additional reading materials: *Kids in the Garden: Growing Plants for Food and Fun* by Elizabeth McCorquodale (Black Dog Publishing, March 2010). This book is filled with fun gardening activities, recipes, and knowledge for kids and their grownups.

CHAPTER TEN

Growing Worms and Vermicompost for Sale

"Fear not, then, thou child infirm;
There's no god dare wrong a worm."
RALPH WALDO EMERSON

Many have turned a hobby into a profitable business, and a worm hobby is no exception. Farming worms can be a viable business venture and offers more than one business option. The worms can be sold for breeding stock to other worm farmers, as a composter, as bait in the fishing industry, or as food to zoos, aquariums, or game breeders. In addition, a business can be formed that strictly sells vermicompost and vermicastings.

While starting a worm farming business might sound like a simple process, there are several factors to consider before getting started. Some things you will need to consider are the process of setting up a business as well as setting up a worm farm on a large scale. This chapter will help you determine if a business in worms is for you and offer suggestions on how to get started.

You might want to create an idea binder for your business. Use a three-ring binder to gather notes and ideas, add photos of vermicomposting products, answer questions in this chapter, and add any other information on running a business that might be pertinent to your project.

Set Up Your Business

The possibilities for a business in vermiculture might include selling worms as breeding stock, for composting, as bait, for food to other animals, and as compost. Determining which one is right for you will require some research and evaluation of your level of commitment to the business. You also will need to determine what type of equipment and tools you would need to operate your business. For example, how many vermicomposting bins will you need to get started? Will you be making them or purchasing ready-made systems?

Being familiar with the process of worm farming is key in starting a business in vermiculture. Once you learn to care for worms on a small-scale, you can start to experiment with producing worms and castings on a larger-scale. The amount of time and materials required on a small-scale will multiply a hundred fold as your business grows.

Some things to consider when venturing into a vermiculture business include:

1. Start with high quality worms. Purchase your startup worms from a reputable dealer to ensure that your worms will be of highest quality stock.

2. Determine what type of worm business you want to have. Do you want to sell vermicompost and castings only? Do you want to be a breeder and sell the worms? Are you interested in selling vermicomposting supplies like bins and bedding? Will education/ classes be part of your business?

3. Do you want to have a storefront? Or sell via the Internet?

4. Where will your business be? Do you have the room in your current location? Or will you need to purchase or rent somewhere larger?

5. Are there other worm-related businesses in your area?

6. What type of experience do you have with worms?

7. How do you plan to operate on a daily basis? Will you be the only one tending to the worms, or will you hire someone?

8. What are the zoning laws where your business will be?

As mentioned, the first step to owning a successful worm business is having quality worms. Make sure you purchase your first batch of worms from a reputable source known for producing high-quality worms that have the characteristics you are looking for. For example, if you are planning to open a vermicastings business, you obviously will need worms that are fast and capable of consuming a great amount of food in order to produce vermicastings at a constant rate. You want to have as many marketable aspects of your worms and of your business as possible. Otherwise, why would someone choose your worms or product over some of the other options out there?

Also, you most likely will want to feed the worms a constant source of nutrients. Compost is fine for your own purposes, but if you want to market your quality castings, you want to say that your worms are feed the best food available. *You can see an example of this in the case study in this chapter.*

If you are going to sell the worms for food, bait, or other purposes, you will want to make sure your worms are a good size. Some worms are even known for being "wigglier" than others, which is a good quality when you are trying to attract a predator.

To sell your worms to those wanting to create their own vermicomposting systems, you will need to keep track of the ages of the worms you are selling so that you can label them as bed-run or breeders. You will see a sample of how to sort your worms in the following case study. However, any system you devise will work as long as you keep your worms sorted and labeled successfully.

For more ideas about how to start and conduct a business involving worms, read the following case study:

CASE STUDY: OPENING A SUCCESSFUL WORM BUSINESS

Becky Jacobs and Debra Slone
Dirty Worms
Ocklawaha, FL
dirtywormsl@yahoo.com
www.dirtyworms.com

Becky Jacobs, her sister Debi Slone, and their brother Gregg Jacobs are co-owners of a worm business based out of Central Florida. They sell worm castings for use in the garden and, occasionally, worms, so patrons can start their own vermicomposting systems. For more information, visit **www.dirtyworms.com***.*

Three years ago, Becky and Debi were looking for a green business that would make them some extra money while helping the environment. But nothing seemed right. Finally, Debi found an advertisement in a local paper about a man who was selling worms for vermicomposting.

"We have all gotten to the point where we want to be in control of our own food and control of what we put into our bodies," Becky said. "And that is kind of the way we see the world going — using fewer chemicals and being a little bit more natural. So, I think as a family we are trying to take on that mind-set and doing our part to play a role in that."

The duo brought their brother and father over to the man's farm to take a tour and meet their newest business partners — the worms. The family started out with nine buckets, about 3,000 worms.

They chose an African Night Crawler to help them get started on their business. "For Florida or these warmer climates, the African Night Crawler is awesome because it can handle a little bit warmer temperatures," Becky said. "Plus, from the reading that I have done, Night Crawlers tend to go deeper in the soil than Red Wigglers — they are shallower worms — so what type of vermicompost setup you are doing may depend on the type of worm you want to use."

Keeping and Feeding the Worms

But there was more to setting up a business than just getting their hands on some worms. They also had to figure out where to keep them comfortably, what to feed them, and how to harvest the vermicastings without hurting their hard-working worm friends.

What developed was not a traditional setup. They keep the worms in 3 ½-gallon buckets stacked up within a 10 by 12-foot shed in their brother's backyard. There are anywhere from 250 to 300 worms in each bucket and about a hundred buckets. They try to keep it at a 78 to 80 degree temperature with air conditioning, fans, and a heating system in the winter.

"The worms stay most active at that temperature," Becky said. "They can handle a little bit higher temperatures or a little bit cooler temperatures, but they are going to kind of go into a hibernation where they are not moving around as much and not eating as much. We try to keep them at their optimal temperature so they are eating; they are pooping; they are mating and laying those eggs, the cocoons."

The worms are separated by age, which makes it easier to keep track of which worms could be sold and which might need a little more food because of their age. The buckets are labeled by the ages of the worms inside.

As for feeding, this is not a typical vermicomposting system. Although the Dirty Worms family fully supports vermicomposting and sells many of their worms to vermicomposters, they do not produce the amount of compost they would need to feed 30,000 worms. Instead, they feed the worms a bedding of Black Gold Peat Bog. They add a grain mix in with the peat, as well as a milk booster to act as a digestive enzyme.

"By doing it this way, it is more controlled so basically it is balanced from harvest to harvest," Becky said. "Every harvest our castings are always about the same level. We will have ours tested at least once a year if not twice a year, and the levels of each of those elements rarely changes that significantly. Because we are selling the castings we want them to be as pure as possible."

The Harvest

A side view of the harvester. The tray on the bottom is the bin holding the worm castings. While in use, the tray is pushed under the cylinder.

So how do Becky and her family harvest the castings in a timely fashion while still keeping all their worms separated and healthy? By creating an ingenious machine they call the harvester. Setting up an assembly-line system that makes sure every member of the family has an important job to complete.

Every two weeks is harvest day. The family starts early on a Saturday morning, and the process can take four hours to most of the day. The worm buckets are taken, one at a time, to the harvester. The harvester is a 10-foot cylinder wrapped with ⅛-inch screen.

When turned on, the machine spins at a very slow speed. The bucket full of worms is dumped into the top of the machine, and the contents are pushed gently toward the end.

Pushing the worms and their surroundings into the harvester

The worm castings fall through the screen into a bin below. The worms and dirt fall into a separate bin at the end of the cylinder, called the refuge.

Becky pours a bucket of dirt into the mixer.

Meanwhile, Becky and her sister Debi prepare the now-empty buckets with the bedding. They mix four buckets of peat into a large barrel that spins — they call it the mixer. They add four cups of the grain and a tablespoon of the milk booster. A little bit of water so the soil will be moist, and you have the mixture for four worm buckets.

However, it is not quite ready for its wiggly consumers. During the mixing process, the mixer tends to pull some of the dirt into chunks, which are difficult for the worms to eat through. So, the Dirty Worms team created yet another machine they call the Eager Beaver: a tiller blade and a lawn mower blade that breaks up the dirt and fluffs it for the worms.

"Whenever we started doing this, it increased our quantity of castings and everything that we were getting out because they literally had more dirt to eat through," Becky said.

Once the buckets are ready and labeled, they are ready to receive their worms.

The buckets are labeled according to how old the worms are.

Debi pouring dirt into the Eager Beaver

Next, the separator, usually Becky's father, picks out the worms from the dirt and worm mixture that fell into the refuge. The refuge will contain cocoons and baby worms that must be placed into special buckets with similarly aged worms. The bulk of the worms will be returned to their bucket to begin the process again.

"You cannot worry about every worm," Becky cautioned. "In the beginning, we worried about every little worm. But what we have learned is you have to ensure you have the proper life cycle going on because if you have that then you are always going to have replacement worms. You just cannot save them all."

Becky's father separates the worms from the dirt so the worms can be placed back in another bucket.

Future Generations — For Sale

The cocoons that Becky's father separates are important to the future of Dirty Worms because they represent the next batch of hard-working worms. The worms lay the most eggs in the fall when it starts cooling off, according to Becky.

Some of Dirty Worms' hard workers. The white spots are worm cocoons.

At this time, they open up their worm castings business into a worm selling business as well. Sometimes, Becky said, they have people who cannot afford a bucket of full-grown worms, so they will buy some baby worms and cocoons instead. They use these new worms to create their own worm bins. It takes about ten to 12 weeks for worm cocoons to hatch and for the baby worms to begin making castings. So, it only takes a couple of months to get a new composting system off the ground.

The family also will sell off some of their older worms in the spring and fall. "Our worms are our workers, so if we sell them all off, then we do not have all of our workers working," Becky said. "But, we hope in the future to be able to grow our worms to the point where we could have a bigger supply of worms, and we also could provide those to people more frequently than just a couple times a year."

Advice on Vermicomposting Systems and Vermicastings

Even though Becky and her family do not use a vermicomposting system in their business, they are advocates of the idea, and they enjoy giving advice to customers who are buying their worms to use in vermicomposting systems.

"Do not make a science out of it," Becky said. "Have fun with it. Think like a worm. Think about the environment the worm wants to be in and try to formulate that environment."

Debi added: "It needs to be a moist area; it needs to be a cool area. Worms are going to burrow under the ground. You are not going to see them constantly, and people will start digging and say, 'Well I do not see any of my worms anymore.' And sand is not the answer."

Some things Debi and Becky warn customers to stay away from are citrus foods and onions. Although worms will eat them, they are not that healthy for the worm and will not give you the nutrients your soil is looking for. "But people are surprised when they hear what all you can put in a compost bin."

Debi said. "Throw your eggshells in there. Throw your newspapers in there."

Some of Dirty Worms' hard workers

And according to Becky, worm castings do not go bad. They can dry out, but they do not lose their nutritional value. And a little bit goes a long way. If you are using the castings themselves, the Dirty Worms team recommends adding a bit of worm castings to a potted plant each season when you re-pot it. Or, you can add the castings directly to your lawn (as long as you do not pile them up — sprinkle them throughout the lawn). The castings will release their nutrients into the soil over time.

According to the Dirty Worms website, although not necessary, plants can be safely grown in 100 percent worm castings. Castings absorb water so you do not have to water as often. And the cylindrical shape of the casting helps to keep the soil loose and allows oxygen to permeate into the soil and into the root system. You also can make worm tea, as is discussed earlier in this book. The Dirty Worms team suggests soaking one part castings in three parts water for 12 to 24 hours. For more ways to use castings, visit **www.dirtyworms.com/how_do_i_use_worm_castings**.

Supply and Demand

And the family's system seems to be working. Out of every bucket, they are able to harvest about two-thirds of it as pure castings. "We average about 750 pounds of castings every harvest," Becky said. "And we have about 100 buckets, so if you divide that through — you know some buckets may give us more castings, some less — but if you divide it through, that is what, about 7 pounds per bucket?"

The collected worm castings

They then sell the castings by the pound as well. They bag the castings in 4-pound, 10-pound, or 25-pound bags. Their most profitable seasons are spring and summer, and over the winter, they usually stockpile the castings for the next year.

Most of the Dirty Worms' sales take place at local farmers markets or by word of mouth. "Some of our prior customers actually do our sales for us," Debi said. "If there is a person there that is trying to understand it, and you are giving your spiel and explaining what castings are, what they do, how to use them, and how wonderful they are, then you will usually have a client, an existing client, walk up behind you and be like, 'You definitely need to get some of this! This works! It is good stuff!' So, they end up helping us sell the product to those who are not familiar with it. But we find that at every show. Every show."

"We were at Dunnellon one time at a show, and it was the end of the day," Becky said. "We had everything packed up and were just about ready to pull out onto the road, and then, this lady pulls into where we were parked, and she is like 'Oh my gosh, I need castings! I got them from you last year, and I have gotta have a bag!' So, we were more than proud to get out of our trucks and get some castings out for her."

Debi added: "And when we were down in The Villages, we had some clients actually come up into that show, and they walked straight to our booth as soon as they walked in. They said, 'This is the only reason we are here. We came to get our castings, and we have got to get going because we have planting to do.'"

Becky and Debi also would like to expand their business into online sales as well. They are setting themselves up to be able to ship worm castings and are planning on adding a lot to their website for national customers. But they want to make sure to keep their prices down, so their worm castings are affordable to the average gardener.

"We do not want somebody to go buy a chemical fertilizer just because it is cheaper," Becky said. "We want to stay somewhat competitive so that they will choose a natural option over that chemical option to stay healthier. I just think it is better for our whole world, you know, for all of us. The more people who use worm castings — it is not just benefiting them, it is benefiting everyone around them."

Business Success Factors

Any new business venture requires six key ingredients, or factors, for its ultimate success. A worm business is no different. Those essential factors to ensure long-term success include:

- Passion is the prime ingredient. A successful worm business is "more than a business" to its owner. Are you passionate about worms and the benefits of gardening with them?

- A solid business foundation is built on a well-considered, strategic plan. Thinking out your plan and fine-tuning the details ahead of time is a key to a successful worm business.

- Excellent customer relations are the hallmark of success in any retail-oriented business.

- Quality, reliability, and service are emphasized.

- Procedures, products, pricing, and all the strategic necessities of the business are regularly evaluated and monitored by the owner.

- A flexible business remains successful as it adapts readily to changes in the industry, technology, and market. Are you knowledgeable about all aspects of a worm business so you can adapt, if needed?

Almost everyone has dreamed of owning his or her own business. Often, these dreams are the result of dealing with difficult bosses, low pay, long hours, swing shifts, and other frustrations that come from working for someone else. In the safe confines of the imagination, the vision of owning a business is immensely satisfying: You are your own boss, you make your own decisions, and you do not have to answer to anyone else. What could be better?

Although there are elements of truth in this dreamworld vision of business ownership, it is also true that in reality, business owners have problems, too. The problems are different from the frustrations faced by employees, but they are serious and stomach-wrenching just the same. You will want to know your personal capacity to deal with the problems of business ownership before you jump out of the workforce and take over the boss's chair.

Some questions to consider that will affect the ultimate success of a worm business might include the following. Grab a pen and paper and honestly answer them to determine your passion for the world of worms.

1. Determine in what form you want to sell your worms — as breeding stock to other worm farmers, as a composter, as bait in the fishing industry, as food to zoos, aquariums, or game breeders, or a combination of all of these options? Or, do you want to sell vermicompost and vermicastings?

2. Why do you want to start a worm business?

3. Can you work long hours without a steady paycheck to get a worm business off the ground?

4. How many hours a week are you able to devote to starting your worm business?

5. Do you have experience running a retail-type business?

6. Who are your customers?

7. How will your customers find your business?

8. Are there any other worm-related businesses in your area? Are they the same or different than yours?

9. Is your yard, basement, or greenhouse large enough to support farming worms in bulk? Or will you need to purchase a greenhouse or rent land?

10. Do you have enough room in your dedicated worm space to sort and package?

11. Do you plan to hire help or do all the work yourself?

12. What items supplies would you need to start your business? Worms, worm housing, feed stock, etc.

13. Where will you store the supplies and products you want to sell?

14. How much money would you need to get your business started?

15. Do you have enough money to get started? Or, would you need to apply for a business loan?

If the answers to these questions have not scared you away yet, it is time to buckle down and do some research to start formulating a plan for your worm business.

Determine Marketability

After you have made sure the idea of a worm business is something you are truly passionate about and is manageable for your lifestyle, you must make sure that you have a marketable idea. You will need to determine whether your worm business is going to make money and if there is even a market for your worm product. Then, you will have to decide if you can reach that market.

Not only do you *need* to have a marketable idea, you also *must* have a way to market or advertise that idea. If no one can find you or knows about you or your product, then you are not going to sell it. Therefore, making sure that you do your research well is crucial. You do not want to start a worm business that is going to be impossible for you to market or advertise. A worst-case scenario would be trying to market worms that no one is interested in buying. This first step is going to save you from any of that.

An easy way to start your search is to look for worm-related businesses on the Internet. Although the Internet is not always reliable and the information may need to be double-checked for accuracy, it is a good place to start. When running your search, you also will find any other business ideas that might be similar to yours. They can be offering the same thing as you, even if it is in a different way. Considering the amount of information and worm-related products out there, you can be certain that there is a market out there for your worm business.

A good way to search for other worm businesses is to use a meta-search engine. This search engine will incorporate more than one search engine for you at once. So, when you put your query in, you will not just be searching on Google®, you will be searching on Yahoo!®, MSN®, and others with one search entry. This is a good time saver and is effective. One option is Dogpile® (**www.dogpile.com**); this site conducts a search and sends it out to a list of search engines that are customizable. The search engine results are displayed on an individual basis. Another meta-search engine that you can try is Yippy™ (**http://search.yippy.com**). When you enter a search term, such as "worms," Vivisimo® (**http://vivisimo.com**) will return matching responses from the major search engines and sort the pages into categories. You also can try **www.mamma.com**®, **www.surfwax.com**®, and **www.metacrawler.com**®.

National research

You will need national research if you plan to open your worm business in a different area of the country. Wherever you decide to do business as a worm farmer, you will need to research local demographics and market conditions. A 2009 issue of *Forbes* magazine noted the transient impulses stimulated by the historic recession, naming its list of the 10 best metro and small metro areas to start a business in. Criteria for the ratings included local cost of doing business, crime rate, education attainment, living costs, projected income and job growth. You also might want to add some local market research on per-capital income levels, housing prices, family sizes, and other factors likely to impact business. Luckily, because worms are easily packaged and shipped, you do not need to live in a large metro area to start a worm farm. In fact, a more rural location might be better considering the nature of the business you are considering starting.

Scouting the competition

Never underestimate the value of knowing your competition. Make a list of the other worm businesses in your market. Which ones target the same population that you will? Find out what they are selling and their prices. For example, is there a nearby bait shop selling worms? How will your business differ from that one? How do your worms compare to theirs?

Take a detailed look at your competition when you narrow down your choices. The information you want can be hard to find. The best way to find information about your competition may be a visit to their establishments or phone them. Be creative and ask a lot of questions.

Other sources of information on competition include the following ideas:

- Telephone book — Will give you the number and location of your competitors

- Chambers of Commerce — They have lists of local businesses. Verify whether it is a complete list, not just Chamber members.

- Local newspapers — Study the local advertisements and help wanted ads.

- Craigslist/eBay — Are there online sources that sell worms or vermicomposting products?

Take notes in your idea binder.

06-10-2015 2:21PM

Item(s) checked out to Grant, Steven A.

TITLE: The complete guide to working wit
BARCODE: 31143009826224
DUE DATE: 07-08-15

Create a Business Plan

Business plans are the road map to success. The only way you can reach your goal of succeeding with your worm business is by having a well-thought-out plan. It is difficult at best to establish and operate a business when you do not quite know how to go about it — let alone trying to accomplish it without a thorough assessment of what you want to accomplish, how you plan to go about it, and what financial support you have to accomplish it.

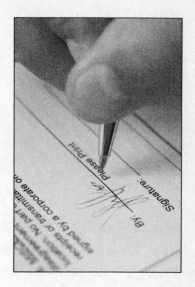

As you prepare to undertake the enormous task of starting a worm business, evaluate your situation as it stands today, and visualize where you want to be three to five years from now. To work your way from today's standpoint to owning and operating a successful worm business, you must set yourself goals to reach along the way that will serve as benchmarks on your road to success. A business plan also will be a key ingredient if you need to apply for a business loan.

The most important and basic information to include in a business plan are:

- Stating your business goals. For example, do you want to sell the worms themselves, vermicastings, worm tea, or all of them?

- Describing the approach you will take to accomplish those goals. Will you sell locally at farmers markets, in a storefront, or via the Internet?

- Discussing what potential problems you may encounter along the way, and how you plan to address those problems. For example, what will you do if your worm stock suddenly dies off?

- Outlining the organizational structure of the business (as it is today and how you plan it to be). Do you plan to run all parts of the business, or hire people now or in the future? Will you handle the marketing aspect as well, or hire an outside company?

- Stating the capital, or cash and goods, you will use to generate income, get started, and to keep in operation.

There are various formats and models available for developing business plans. Entire books are devoted to guiding you through the development of a business plan. However, before you constrain yourself to any one business plan format, consider that a business plan should be as unique as the business for which it is being written. No two businesses are the same, and even though there may be some basic similarities, each business is as individual and unique as a person. Therefore, even though it is recommended that you follow the basic structure of commonly used templates, you should customize your worm business plan to fit your needs. A number of websites provide you with a variety of samples and templates that can also be used as reference, such as **www.bplans.com**, **www.nebs.com/nebsEcat/business_tools/bptemplate**, and **www.planmagic.com**, to name a few.

When writing your business plan, stay focused on its ultimate purpose and consider the many reasons why the plan is developed and its possible applications. For instance, if you do not have a loan proposal — essentially a condensed version of the business plan used by businesses to request financing — when trying to secure financing for your business, business plans are great supporting documentation to attach to a loan application.

Plans also are used as a means of introducing your business to a new market or presenting your business to a prospective business partner or investor.

Parts of a business plan

Business plans vary in style and format, but most include the following sections:

- Cover page
- Table of contents
- Mission statement
- Executive summary
- Description of proposed business
- Management and staffing
- Market analysis
- Industry background
- Target market
- Product description
- Market approach strategy
- Marketing
- Operations
- Strengths and weaknesses
- Financial projections
- Conclusion
- Supporting documents

A sample Worm Vermiculture business plan is available in the Appendix.

Cover Page

The cover page should be evenly laid out with all the information centered on the page. Always write the name of your company in all capital letters in the upper half of the page. Several line spaces down, write the title "Business Plan." Last, write your company's address, the contact person's name (your name).

Table of Contents

The table of contents will include a list of the remaining items in the document with page numbers.

Body of the Business Plan

Mission Statement

It is very important that you present your worm business and what it is all about from the beginning of your business plan. A mission statement is only as significant as you intend it to be. However, it should be written and placed in important documents and ultimately used as a beacon that will always guide you to where you intend your business to go. When writing your mission statement, three key elements that must be considered and discussed are: the purpose of your worm business, the goods or services you provide, and a statement regarding your company's attitude toward your employees and customers. A well-written mission statement could be as short as one paragraph but should not be longer than two.

Executive Summary

The executive summary should be about one to two pages long and should actually be written last, as it is a summary of all the information you have included in the plan. It should address what your worm market is, the purpose of the business, where it will be located, and how it will be managed. Write the executive summary in such a way that it will prompt the reader to look deeper into the business plan. It is a good idea to discuss the various elements of your worm business plan in the order you address them in the rest of the document.

Description Of Proposed Vermiculture Business

Describe in detail the purpose for which the business plan is being written. State what you intend to accomplish. Describe your goods, services, and the role your worm business will play in the overall global market. Explain what makes your worm business different from all the rest in the same arena. Clearly identify the goals and objectives of your business. The average length for the proposed business description section should be one to two pages but will vary based on the specifics of your worm business idea.

Management And Staffing

Clearly identifying the management team and any other staff that may be part of the everyday operations of the business will strengthen your business viability by demonstrating that the business will be well managed. Keep in mind that a company's greatest asset is its employees. State who the owners of the business are, as well as other key employees with backgrounds in the vermiculture business. Identify the management talent you have on board (this may include yourself) as well as any others you may need in the future to expand your business. For instance, it may just be yourself when starting up; however, in your plans for expansion, you might think about incorporating someone well versed in vermiculture. The management and staffing section of the plan could be as short as one paragraph if you are the only employee or it could be as long as a page or two, depending on how many people you have and anticipate having as part of your staff.

Market Analysis

The market analysis section should include the various types of worm businesses. If you are new to the industry, do your research and include information that you have acquired through research and data collection. Numerous sources of information are available, both online and through printed media, which can provide you with a wealth of knowledge about worms as a business. This process will add validity to your presentation, and you will be better prepared to answer any questions that may be presented to you. Essential elements to include in this section include other worm businesses that you might expand into and possible needs, a description of your products or services, your competition, and your planned strategy and approach to the market.

Market Your Business

Your marketing plan targets of all of the potential customers who will purchase your product or service. It is a study of your target market: who is buying, why they are buying, and how you will surpass the competition and get that market to buy from you. Your plan should also cover how you plan to get the products to your customers, including the details of packaging and distributing them to the market.

Marketing plan worksheet

Who are your customers going to be?

_____

_____

Who are your competitors?

_____

_____

How can you compete in this market?

_____

_____

What are your strengths and weaknesses in comparison to competitors?

_____

_____

What can you do better than your competitors?

_____

_____

Are there any governmental or legal factors affecting your vermiculture business?

_____

_____

What advantages does your product have over the competition?

_____

_____

What type of image do you want for your product?

_____

_____

What features will be emphasized?

_____

_____

What is your pricing strategy?

_____

_____

Is your pricing in line with your image?

_____

_____

Do your prices properly cover costs?

_____

_____

What types of promotion will you use? (Television, radio, direct mail, personal contacts, newspaper, magazines, yellow pages, billboard, Internet, classifieds, and trade associations.)

_____

_____

Industry Background

Focus on the segment of the market that you will be a part of. Include trends and statistics that reflect the direction the market is going and how you will fit into that movement. Discuss major changes that have taken place in the vermiculture industry in the recent past, which will affect how you will conduct business. Provide a general overview of your projected customer base, such as wholesalers or domestic consumers. Great sources to research online are The U.S. Customs and Border Protection (**www.cbp.gov**), the World Trade Organization (**www.wto.org**), U.S. International Trade Commission (**www.usitc.gov**), and the International Trade Administration (**www.trade.gov**). Be sure to research if it is viable to ship worms outside the country.

Target Market

The target market is who your customer, or groups of customers, will be. By this point, you already would have decided on the role you will take on; so, it is a good idea to narrow down your proposed customer base to a reasonable volume. If you try to spread your possibilities too thin, you may be wasting your time on efforts that will not pay off and end up missing some real possibilities. Identify the characteristics of the principal market you intend to target, such as demographics, market trends, and geographic location of the market.

Expand your discussion to include the avenues you will use to reach your market. Include whether you plan to use the Internet, printed media, trade shows, and such. Trade shows are exhibitions organized with the purpose of providing a venue where companies can showcase their products and services. Or it might be as simple as your local farmers market.

Product Description

Do not just describe your product or service — describe it as it will benefit or fill the needs of potential customers, and center your attention on where you have a clear advantage. Elaborate on what your vermiculture products or services are.

Market Approach Strategy

How do you anticipate entering such the worm market? Do you anticipate carving out a niche? Determining how to enter the market and what strategy to use will be critical for breaking into the market.

Products and Services

This section will focus on the uniqueness of your products or services and how your potential customers will benefit from them. Describe in detail the services your business provides, how the services are provided, and what makes the services you provide unique and different from other worm businesses that provide the same service or deal with the same goods, i.e. worms or worm castings. Address the benefits of using your services or buying your goods instead of those of the competitors. For example, are your worms kept in the best environment? How do your worms stand out over those for sale at the local bait shop, for example?

Pricing Strategy

The pricing strategy segment is about determining how to price your products or services in such a way that it will allow you to remain competitive while still making a reasonable profit. You will be better off setting realistic prices rather than pricing yourself out of the market and losing money by pricing your goods or services too high. Therefore, you must take extreme care when pricing your goods and services. The most effective method of doing this is by gauging your costs, estimating the tangible benefits to your customers, and making a comparison of your goods, services, and prices to similar ones on the market.

A good rule to follow is to set your price by considering how much the goods or services cost you, and then add what you think would be a fair price for the benefits the goods or services will provide to the customer. Keep in mind that when you are determining your cost of the goods or services, you must consider all the costs, such as freight costs, the cost of labor and materials, selling costs, and administrative costs.

Sales and Distribution

Now that you have determined how to price your goods and services, it is time to think about how you are going to sell and distribute your products and services. Describe the system you will use for processing orders, shipping the goods, and billing your customers. Also, address what methods of payment will be acceptable from your customers, including credit terms and discounts. In regard to the actual distribution of the goods, discuss the methods of distribution you anticipate using, as well as the anticipated costs associated with it. There are several methods of distribution to choose from, such as direct mail, telemarketing, wholesale outlets, retail stores, or via a website on the Internet. How will you store your worms/worm products before selling? Is there a special way you will have to ship the product? What are the regulations for shipping live animals like worms?

Advertising and Promotion

Discuss how you plan to advertise your products and services through market-specific channels, such as magazines or the Internet. Promote your business to a specific market. One of your goals in this section is to break down what percentage of your advertising budget will be spent in which media. For instance, the cost of advertising through trade magazines, trade shows, and via an Internet site differs significantly, and the return on your investment on each one of those may not be worth what you spent. Therefore, it is wise to evaluate your advertising and promotion plans carefully before putting them into effect.

Operations

Under the operations section, discuss all aspects of management and manufacturing operations, distribution of goods, and logistics services provided. Logistics is the storage and movement of goods from their original location to their final destination. Concentrate your discussion on how to improve resources in operations and production, which will facilitate the success of the company. Remember that all of the information outlined in this section needs to be backed by realistic numbers, such as cost of buildings, machinery, and equipment, as well as salaries and such.

Discuss the business's current and proposed location, describing in detail any existing facilities. Include a discussion of any equipment you currently have or require in order to expand, and describe the methods you use or anticipate using in your manufacturing and distribution operation. If you have employees, or anticipate having them, give a brief description of the tasks the employees will perform in processing the goods, if manufacturing, or other duties to be performed by the administration team. Will you feed all the worms yourself? Will you hire someone? Where will you get your feedstock to feed the worms? Purchased from the Internet? Collected from local restaurants?

Strengths And Weaknesses

As it is the case in most industries, the competition is tough with numerous business owners in the market, all competing for the same prospects. Those who can take better advantage of their strengths and work in overcoming their weaknesses are the ones who will get ahead of the game. In this section of the plan, elaborate on the particulars of your business that have enabled you, and will continue to enable you, to be successful. Discuss those things that set you apart and give you an advantage over your competitors, such as your particular geographic location, the unique worm farming setup, the superior organic food fed to your worms, etc.

There are no strengths without weaknesses, and as hard as it may be to face and deal with those weaknesses that could be holding you back, addressing them will actually help you either to overcome them or deal with them better. Remember that having weaknesses is not a problem only your business faces, because in reality, your competitors have weaknesses to deal with as well. Some weaknesses you may be dealing with at the time you are writing the business plan may be due to inexperience and limited exposure to the market, both of which you can overcome. However, some weaknesses that you cannot overcome, but must be dealt with head-on, are issues such as threats to your products caused by environmental concerns and other regulatory issues. Each of the weaknesses identified must be discussed in detail as to how you plan to overcome the particular weakness or how you foresee ultimately eliminating it. Although important, discussing strengths and weaknesses should not take away from other focal points of the business plan. Therefore, keep this section relatively short, no more than one page in length.

Conclusion

The conclusion is the last written element of the business plan. Make use of this last opportunity to state your case wisely and highlight key issues discussed in the plan. Then, wrap it up, and close with a summary of your plans for the expansion and progress of your business. Use language that will help the reader visualize what you will be able to accomplish and how successful your business will be should you receive the support you are requesting. Remember, you will be using this business plan to apply for any business loans or to register and prove you are a legitimate business in the eyes of the law.

Supporting Documents

Attaching supporting documentation to your business plan certainly will strengthen it and make it more valuable. However, do not overburden it with too many attachments; finding a balance is important. Before you start attaching documents, ask yourself if that particular piece of information will make a difference — if the answer is no, then leave it out. Documents that you should attach include:

- Copies of the business principals' résumés
- Tax returns and personal financial statements of the principals for the last three years
- A copy of licenses, certifications, and other relevant legal documents
- A copy of the lease or purchase agreement, if you are leasing or buying space
- Copies of letters of intent from suppliers (if applicable)

Determine the Legal Structure of Your Business

Deciding which legal structure you would like to build your vermiculture business under will be the backbone of your operation. The legal structure of your business will set the platform for your everyday operations, as it will influence the way you proceed with financial, tax, and legal issues — just to name a few. It even will play a part in how you name your company, as you will be adding Inc., Co., LLC, and such at the end of the name to specify what type of company you are. It will dictate what type of documents need to be filed with the different governmental agencies, and how much and what type of documentation you will need to make accessible for public scrutiny. In addition, it will define how you actually will operate your business. To assist you in determining how you want to operate your business, here is a chart that overviews the differences. You also might want to check with your local town, city, and state for details and benefits of each.

Business Entity Chart

Legal entity	Costs involved	Number of owners	Paperwork	Tax implications	Liability issues
Sole proprietorship	Local fees assessed for registering business; generally between $25 and $100	One	Local licenses and registrations; assumed name registration	Owner is responsible for all personal and business taxes.	Owner is personally liable for all financial and legal transactions.
Partnership	Local fees assessed for registering business; generally between $25 and $100	Two or more	Partnership agreement	Business income passes through to partners and is taxed at the individual level only.	Partners are personally liable for all financial and legal transactions, including those of the other partners.
LLC	Filing fees for articles of incorporation; generally between $100 and $800, depending on the state	One or more	Articles of organization; operating agreement	Business income passes through to owners and is taxed at the individual level only.	Owners are protected from liability; company carries all liability regarding financial and legal transactions.
Corporation	Varies with each state, can range from $100 to $500	One or more; must designate directors and officers	Articles of incorporation to be filed with state; quarterly and annual report requirements; annual meeting reports	Corporation is taxed as a legal entity; income earned from business is taxed at individual level.	Owners are protected from liability; company carries all liability regarding financial and legal transactions.

Sole proprietorship

Sole proprietorship is the most prevalent type of legal structure adopted by startup or small businesses, and it is the easiest to put into operation. It is a type of business owned and operated by one owner, and it is not set up as any kind of corporation. Therefore, you will have absolute control of all operations. Under a sole proprietorship, you own 100 percent of the business, its assets, and its liabilities. Some of the disadvantages are that you are wholly responsible for securing all monetary backing, and you are ultimately responsible for any legal actions against your business. However, it has some great advantages, such as being relatively inexpensive to set up, and with the exception of a couple of extra tax forms, there is no requirement to file complicated tax returns in addition to your own personal tax returns. Also, as a sole proprietor, you can operate under your own name or you can choose to conduct business under a fictitious name. Most vermiculture business owners who start small begin their operations as sole proprietors and then evaluate a change later as the business grows, expands, and changes.

General partnership

A partnership is almost as easy to establish as a sole proprietorship, with a few exceptions. In a partnership, all profits and losses are shared between or among the partners. In a partnership, not all partners necessarily have equal ownership of the business. Normally, the extent of financial contributions toward the business determines the percentage of each partner's ownership. This percentage relates to sharing the organization's revenues as well as its financial and legal liabilities. One key difference between a partnership and a sole proprietorship is that the business does not cease to exist with the death of a partner. Under such circumstances, the deceased partner's share can either be taken over by a new partner, or the partnership can be reorganized to accommodate the change. In either case, the business is able to continue without much disruption.

Although not all entrepreneurs benefit from turning their sole proprietorship businesses to partnerships, some thrive when incorporating partners into the business. In such instances, the business benefits significantly from the knowledge and expertise each partner contributes toward the overall operation of the business. As your business grows, it might be advantageous for you to come together in a partnership with someone who is knowledgeable in the collection field and will be able to contribute toward the expansion of the operation. Sometimes, as a sole proprietorship grows, the needs of the company outgrow the knowledge and capabilities of the single owner and require the input of someone who has the knowledge and experience necessary to take the company to its next level.

When establishing a partnership, it is in the best interest of all partners involved to have an attorney develop a partnership agreement. Partnership agreements are simple legal documents that normally include information such as the name and purpose of the partnership, the legal address of the business, how long the partnership is intended to last, and the names of the partners. It also addresses each partner's contribution both professionally and financially and how profits and losses will be distributed. A partnership agreement also needs to disclose how changes in the organization will be addressed, such as death of a partner, the addition of a new partner, or the selling of one partner's interest to another individual. The agreement ultimately must address how the assets and liabilities will be distributed, should the partnership dissolve.

Ways to Finance a Business

As stated earlier in this chapter, one of the primary purposes of a business plan for your worm venture is to use it as a tool to obtain financing for the business. When it comes to obtaining the money you need to start and operate a vermiculture business, you have numerous options that extend beyond obtaining a bank loan or traditional business financing. Some of the sources of funding include:

- **Personal Savings** — Especially for sole business owners, the primary source for business financing comes from your own personal savings or the money of each of the business owners.

- **Borrow it** — Money can be borrowed from banks, financial institutions, family members, and friends.

- **Sell it** — Selling a part of your company to investors can provide needed capital, but sharing ownership has its drawbacks.

- **Pledge it** — Private or public business development grants are available based upon your ability and willingness to "give back" to the community.

- **Share it** — Find a sponsor (coach), employer, business, or individual who will subsidize your business with the goal of enhancing his or her financial gains.

Examining your vermiculture business and discovering your entrepreneurial style are the first steps to finding the funding that matches your company's needs. When the need for money arises, entrepreneurs can become consumed by raising capital. Their judgment becomes clouded and their decision-making ability compromised. The cliché "the end justifies the means" is not always true. Your first step in exploring your financing options is to determine what you are willing to sacrifice and the most efficient and cost-effective way to obtain the money you need.

Available financial sources

The following sections outline the types of financing available to businesses. Making the decision to start or expand a small business opens up a variety of considerations and options. Many burgeoning companies spend far too much time chasing down funds from sources that do not mesh with their business and goals for the business. Finding the right financing options or the wrong financing options can draw the line between the success of your vermiculture business and running into serious problems down the road.

Give it: Your personal investment

Investors and lenders tend to expect you to provide a significant amount of the capital necessary to launch or expand your business. When an entrepreneur puts assets on the line, it sends the message that he or she is committed to making the company a success, which also makes it easier to acquire supplemental funding from outside sources. (There are a few exceptions, such as seed money programs created to assist economically disadvantaged at-risk individuals.) It is recommended that you have enough money put away in a savings account to cover all of your living expenses for a three-year period in case it takes that long for your business to start turning a profit.

Investing your money

Nearly 80 percent of entrepreneurs rely on personal savings to begin a new enterprise. Using personal savings secures the entrepreneur's control and ownership of the business. Because it is your money, no debt is incurred and future profits are not shared with investors.

Converting personal assets to business use is the same as giving your business cash. Not only will you avoid purchasing these assets, but you also will be able to depreciate them. Your accountant will set up the conversion and depreciation schedules. If you have an accountant — and if you do not, think about employing one — they can explain these terms further. Depreciation is the method used to determine the value left in an item. For many people, their greatest personal asset is their home.

Lines of credit, refinancing, and home equity loans often are used to gather up the seed money for launching a new business. Raising cash this way can be risky because it puts your home up as collateral for obtaining the loan. If you default on the loan, it can mean the loss of your home. Personal credit cards, signature loans, and loans against insurance policies and retirement accounts are other common ways of raising startup capital from personal assets you already own.

Home equity loans

Before deciding a home equity loan is a viable financing option, you first have to determine how much equity you have built up in your home. You can estimate this figure using one of a couple of different options. First, you can hire an appraiser, which can cost anywhere from to $275 to upwards of $500 to determine the market value of your home. You then need to subtract any existing mortgage balances from the value. The difference between these two numbers is the total amount of equity you have in the home. Another option for determining the market value of the home is to work with a real estate agent. An agent can use the sales prices of comparable homes in your area to estimate the value of the home.

Two types of equity options exist. One is a home equity loan, which works similarly to a traditional mortgage. You receive the amount of the loan in a lump sum and start paying interest on the loan amount right away. The second option is a home equity line of credit, which is a revolving line of credit that works like a credit card. You can access the money on the line, up to line amount, as you need it. You only pay interest on the outstanding balance. As you use and pay back the amount you use, the line is available for you to use again.

If you decide on accessing the equity in your home, fees might be associated with establishing the loan. Some of the fees you should be aware of include:

- **Appraisal fees** — The fee a professional appraiser charges to determine the market value of your home

- **Origination fees** — The fee paid to the establishment or individual processing the loan. It is the fee a lender charges to process the loan.

- **Title fees** — Fees associated with conducting a title search on the home and/or renewing the title insurance policy to cover the new loan

- **Stamp duties** — Taxes applied to a legal document such as the deed

- **Arrangement fees** — The commitment fee payable to the lender of the loan in order to reserve the mortgage funds

- **Closing fees** — Costs incurred during the loan process that are paid at the end of the transaction

- **Early payoff fee** — Fees that can be required if you pay off the loan early, typically within the first five years of acquiring the loan

If you own your home outright, you can refinance without staking all the equity you have in your home, which leaves room for future refinancing should something go wrong. If you own 20 percent or less in equity, you should never consider borrowing against that. The funds you gain will be minimal, and the second lender will not hesitate to foreclose should trouble arise. To determine feasibility of a home equity loan, follow these steps:

1. Get your home appraised. If the value has increased, you might own more equity than you think.

2. Figure out exactly how much you still owe on your mortgage.

3. Take the appraisal valuation and subtract your debt to determine the amount of equity.

4. Figure out your percentage by dividing your equity amount by the valuation amount. If it is less than 50 percent, you should find a different source of capital for your business.

5. If your equity is more than 50 percent, you might be in business. Now is the time to get loan quotes.

6. Figure out how your business plan will be affected by this cash infusion, and make projections for how long it will take for the loan to be paid off.

For example, if the market value of your home is $200,000 and your first mortgage balance is only $100,000, then you only owe 50 percent of the value of the home. This means you have equity built up in your home that you can access to help pay for the startup or operating expenses of the business. As an added bonus, the interest you pay on a mortgage for a primary residence is fully tax deductible. Check with your tax adviser to verify this for your personal financial situation.

Pay down the principal balance of the debt in order to get out of debt faster and regain the equity on your home.

Leveraging your credit

Leveraging your personal credit worthiness is another way to support your business. Because a new business does not have established credit or a credit history, you might be able to leverage your personal credit by guaranteeing the business loan or credit account. Talk with your attorney about personal liability issues for any business debts you acquire. Part of this protection depends on the type of legal entity you establish for the business, such as corporation over a sole proprietorship.

Borrow it: Loans to repay

Borrowing money for business can save the business or be its downfall. When looking at various types of loans, consider such issues as collateral required, interest rates, and repayment terms. **Collateral** is the promise of a specific piece of property to a lender to facilitate repayment. **Interest rates** are the rates at which the borrow pays for the use of funds he or she borrows from a lender. The terms a borrower agrees to when the loan is acquired are the **repayment terms**.

> **WARNING:** If you ever hear anyone use the word **usury**, be careful. The word originally meant charging interest on a loan, but today it is used to describe an unlawful rise in interest charged on a loan or charging an excessive interest rate that is drastically higher than the market rate.

Loans from family and friends

Asking for help from those closest to you can be another smart move when looking for capital. Because you already have a relationship with friends and family, there are no questions of trust, and a willingness to help already exists.

Interest-free or low-interest loans from relatives or friends can help a startup business gain important supplemental capital without having to take out a bank loan or relinquish control and profits of the business to investors.

When considering these investors, ask yourself five questions:

1. Will this person be able to ride out the highs and lows without extensive panicking?

2. Does this person understand the risks and benefits?

3. Will this person want to take control or become problematic?

4. Would a failure ruin your relationship?

5. Does this person bring something to the table, besides cash, that can benefit you and the company?

Lines of credit

Tempting sources of short-term borrowing for small businesses are microloans. These alternative loans are often safer and have lower interest rates. They can help fill the gap between expenditures incurred while acquiring debt accounts to collect on and actually collecting the debt payments. Lines of credit are useful for making sure payroll is met and that the short-term operating costs are covered during the gap.

Sell it: Shared ownership

Investors are a type of owner, which means you must be willing to "sell" a portion of your business and future profits in return for an investor providing you with the money you need up front to start the business or to expand it. Some investors are active participants in daily operations, while others act as silent partners. Silent investors put the money up for the business based on a solid business plan, but they do not get involved in the daily operations of the business.

Creating an Effective Brand

As a small business owner, it may seem that branding your business or yourself just may be a slick advertising move. However, branding your small business is more about positioning your business and yourself in a positive light, so your target market can see your business is the best choice above the others. A brand is the collection of distinctive qualities that facilitate the recognition of your business with potential customers. When you build a business brand, it is not only about what you do — it is also about the benefits your customer will receive from you that they would not receive from another company. Your goal is to keep your customers coming back and to renew your contracts with them year after year.

A brand helps you organize the full range of your marketing and advertising strategies. It will convey what you stand for and who you are. An effective brand will encompass the whole business and will include a special logo that will be everywhere in the business: on stationery, cards, packaging, signs, and more. This brand also will fit right in the pricing of the services or products, customer services, and your business's guarantees.

A brand can benefit the operation of your business by:

- Building strong customer loyalty

- Bringing more credibility to any project

- Delivering your company message fast and effectively

- Hitting an emotional level with people

- Separating yourself and your business from the competition

- Positioning a focused message in both the heart and mind of your target market

- Bringing consistency to your marketing promotions and campaigns

Getting started

How do you go about creating a winning brand that will help customers identify your business with everything that will make them feel comfortable and confident with you? Here are a few suggestions to get you started:

- Identify your personal and business values. Begin to construct this by listing both personal and business values (honesty, quality, and so on). Then create a "value statement" for your business based on this list. Keep it short. The more condensed your value statement is, the easier it will be for you to recall. In addition, the condensed value statement may be the perfect phrase to use as an advertising tag line that will appear on your marketing materials.

- Create a mission statement. A mission statement lays out the purpose underlying your work. A good mission statement is meaningful, but still short enough to remember.

- Create a vision statement. A good vision statement will specify how you will know when you have achieved the goal of your mission statement. Setting targets for yourself and then continually striving to meet them, helps keep you working smarter and remaining innovative as new possibilities open up.

- Identify your starting point. Where are you right now in relation to where you want to be? Write down some of the steps you already know are necessary to make your business dreams become real.

- Describe your market. Understanding whom you want to reach with branding is critical, since choices of advertising, marketing, and other types of publicity will vary depending on the target market(s) you select.

- Create a positioning statement. Positioning is your attempt to control the image of the business your customer will see. What is the impression you hope to make in the mind of your ideal customer? In your community, will you aim to be the lowest-cost provider? The top-quality provider? The most friendly, reliable provider?

Name your business for appeal and recognition

Ideally, the name of your business captures its essence. There are pros and cons for using your name for your business. When you share your name and identity with your company, you create a personal connection with your clients and with your target market. You also use your personal reputation and community image to help build up your business.

The naming process takes place after you have determined the structure of the business you are proposing. You will want to be sure the name you select is legal and accurately reflects what your business does. Verify that no other business in your area shares the name you are considering. Look in your phonebook or online to find out if another business already goes by the name you are considering. You may have to file your name with your state or local government for approval. You may not legally call yourself "Worm's the Word," if you do not have a license.

Avoid long, hard-to-remember names. You may brainstorm business name ideas with friends, business advisers, or others. Think not only of how the name will sound when you answer the phone but also how it will look on a flier or other advertising. Reserve the URL or Web address of your website as soon as you choose a business name, even if you do not plan to set the website up for a few months. Also, you might want to check the availability of selected Web addresses before you settle on a name.

While calling your business by the owner's name is a common approach, "Melissa's Worms" is descriptive but boring. You may want to go beyond the obvious. If so, it is fine to explore your creativity. If you are unsure how to come up with a creative name, get out the yellow pages and look at the wide variety of names for hair salons, restaurants, or other businesses. Pick out your favorites, and then try to understand why they appeal to you. Ask outsiders — friends, relatives, professional advisers — what they think of your ideas, and if they have suggestions. You want to avoid being too "cute" or unprofessional, while still being memorable. When coming up with a name for a vermiculture business, consider using the word worm or other related term in it so customers can have a basic understanding of what your business does. For example, "Worms 'R Us" or "Castings Call for Worms."

Develop your logo

The logo is a visual symbol of your business and your brand. There are many different considerations when choosing a logo or having one designed for you. You probably will want to keep it graphically simple, so it can be enlarged or made smaller, yet remain easily recognizable. A professional graphic designer may be helpful in preparing the symbol for use in multiple formats. It should look as good on a billboard as it does on your truck, an invoice statement, or your business cards.

You also will want to think ahead to the cost of reproducing your logo. Ideally, it will look good in black and white as well as in color because color printing costs more, and you may want to conserve costs at some point. If it renders well in blacks and grays, it will deliver that much more punch when you can afford to print it in color.

The combined effect of your values statement, mission statement, vision, and position statement, plus your definition of market, your business name, and your logo will become, over time, the foundation of your brand. Your unique "business personality" will be presented to the target market through business cards, fliers, brochures, online ad mediums, the yellow pages, and possibly newspaper, radio, or TV advertising. If you develop unified themes and are consistent in presenting your business message and image, your brand will grow with you as your customer list increases. People will know who you are and what you represent. Including clues to the hardest workers of your business, the worms, should be consistent throughout your company's message. That consistent, positive message will greatly increase your chances for profits and long-term success.

Business cards

You must have business cards. A simple, clear design with your name, title, contact information, website, and the logo of your company on the front of it. Hand them out everywhere. Pin them up on bulletin boards. Have them handy whenever you are in a public place, at a trade show, in the home improvement store, or wherever people gather. Prepare your elevator speech (a 30-second rapid fire description of what your business does) and be ready to deliver that speech, with a card, at every opportunity. The more people know who you are and what you do, the more business you will get.

Also, be sure to maximize the space you have on your business cards, which means using both the front and the back of the card. The front of the card can contain all of the contact information for the business, and the back of the card can provide additional information, such as the specific services or items you sell. For example, if you sell worms or their castings, that information can go on the back. Or you could even write a sentence or two on the vermicomposting cycle. Provide enough information on your business card so it acts as a stand-alone seller for your business. This means that if someone were to find your card on the street or on a bulletin board, they could get up to speed quickly on exactly what your business does and how it benefits them to contact you.

You have a variety of ways you can design and print business cards for your worm business. The most expensive way to obtain business cards is to hire a graphic designer to design the business cards and then send the file off to a printer to have the cards printed. Websites such as Vistaprint (**www.vistaprint.com**) and 48hourprint.com (**www.48hourprint.com**) bring customized and professionally printed business cards down an expense level. These sites have professionally designed business card templates you can customize, personalize, and print at a reduced rate. You also have the option to upload your own design, so even if you have a graphic designer create the card, you can print your card through one of these companies for less than most local printers will charge.

Desktop publishing programs also make business card templates available for you to create business cards. You can print these cards on your own printer using business card stock available at any major office supply or stationary store. Although this might be the least expensive way to get the business cards you need, it does require a time investment. Another disadvantage to creating and printing your own business cards is that it might cheapen the image of your company.

CHAPTER ELEVEN

Marketing your Worm Business Via the Internet

"Do ye not comprehend that we are worms born to bring forth the angelic butterfly that flieth unto judgment without screen?"

DANTE ALIGHIERI

Maintaining a website for your business is crucial. Most people searching for a business in their area will start with an Internet search. Give your clients information and a reason to use your services. This chapter outlines the basic components of a website, how to hire a Web page designer, how to use it to your business's advantage, and the fundamentals of SEO. Remember to update your site continually with fresh information, new pictures, updated contact information, and new design features.

Website Design Fundamentals

There are two basic components to a website. They are your Web pages, the compilation of HTML pages you have designed, and the images, content, and other information that will be displayed on your pages. Your individual Web pages collectively create your website. It can be as small as one page, or it can be thousands of pages. All websites have a home page. The home page is the page that site visitors are taken to when they type in your website domain name into a browser. From your home site, visitors can navigate and visit other Web pages on your site.

All websites consistently change as new content and other Web pages are added; so while you may complete your initial design and publish your Web page, typically your site will require further maintenance, updating, and revisions. The most challenging part of creating a website is developing a blueprint for how you want your site organized, what pages it will contain, how content will be organized, and how your pages will be laid out in relation to others as you design your navigation and page relationships. Design your pages individually, formulate what each page should include, and then you can flesh out the actual content and site design later. You can do this work on a piece of paper or even with sticky notes on the wall, since this will help you visualize the layout.

One of the first things to recognize when building a website is that you either will need some type of software program, or you will have to learn HTML coding and build your site from the ground up. For those determined to learn all of the coding necessary to build and maintain a website, these options will be explored later in the book, as well as a variety of software options to help you with your design goals. Starting out with the availability of adding interactive content and items to your website is the best route to take because even if you do not plan to use them in the beginning, you most likely will use them down the road. When approaching your website design, it is usually best to keep colors and fonts at a basic level.

Four main components of a website

1. **Domain name:** This name is registered and corresponds with where your website is physically located on a Web server. It is also used for your email accounts.

2. **Web hosting:** This is the physical "storage" of your Web pages on a server that is connected to the Internet. This machine "serves" your Web pages as they are requested by a Web browser, and this machine has an IP address. The domain name system (DNS) translates your domain name into your Web account IP address and serves up the appropriate Web pages as requested. Your domain registry will store the IP address of your DNS. The concept may be difficult to understand; however, it is actually quite simple. Your website consists of a series of Web pages. These Web pages are files, which are stored on a Web server along with images and other content on a Web server. This Web server has an IP address that is a unique machine name for that Web server. DNS servers translate your domain name (i.e. "www.wormstheword.com") into the IP address where your site actually is hosted, and your Web server then serves your page to the Web browser of your site visitor. Therefore, it is critical that your DNR account (the company where you bought

your domain name) is updated with the physical IP address of your DNS (provided by your hosting company). This ensures that anyone who searches or types in your domain name into a browser window will be directed to the DNS, which then translates this to the IP address of your site and ensures your Web pages are properly displayed at all times.

3. **Web pages**: These are the Web pages you create and publish to your Web server. You can create Web pages with programs such as Microsoft® Office FrontPage, Microsoft Expression Web, Adobe Dreamweaver®, and many other applications, including free design applications.

4. **Optional items**: These might include shopping carts, forms, or databases. Although none of these are required for Web, you will find your needs may change over time, so keep that in mind during the planning process.

Hire a Web designer

A professional website can cost $3,500 to $15,000. This money buys layout, design, copywriting, programming, and the first year of hosting. Keep these suggestions in mind if you decide to hire a Web designer:

- You can find a Web designer online
  - Search for "Web design [your city name]" or "worm business Web design" for people with experience designing insert type of service sites.

- Look at competing worm business sites

  - When you find a design you like, contact the webmaster. The webmaster usually is listed at the bottom of the home page.

  - Visit sites and take notes about what you like and what you do not like.

- Review designers' portfolios and samples

  - Do they grab your attention?

  - Do the links work, and do the graphics load quickly?

  - Is it immediately obvious what the site is promoting?

Domain Names

You must own your own domain name if you want to have a serious Web presence. Your domain name is your brand name on the Web. It is the address every site visitor will type in to visit your website, and it is critical that you choose a good domain name and host it with a reputable provider. You can purchase domain names from dozens of companies. Most offer convenient control panels that let you update settings, including DNS server IP addresses. If you have your own company exchange server, you also will be able to change IP addresses for your mail servers if you do not wish to use the provided POP, or post office protocol, email accounts with your hosting account. This will also allow you to update your contact information, name, address, and email addresses.

Your domain name should identify your business uniquely. The general rule is that the shorter the domain name, the better, and it should be relevant to your company name, service, or products. If you already have an established corporate name or identity, you should try to base your domain name on that corporate identity. This will allow customers to identify your company name with your domain name. For example, Atlantic Publishing Group, Inc.'s domain name is **www.atlantic-pub.com**. You also should secure any similar domain names, the main reason being to protect your identity from others who may use a similar sounding or identical domain name with a different extension. So if you had purchased "www.wormstheword.com," you would also want to grab "www.wormword.com," "www.wormstheword.net," and "www.wormsthewordinc.com." Your primary domain name should be the domain name that is "hosted," while others may be parked at no additional cost and pointed to the main domain name URL. This way, you only pay for one hosted domain name but can use many domain names on the Internet, all directing site visitors to your main hosted site.

It is important that you name your website after your domain name. The primary reason for this is so that people know your website and business by name. CNN[SM] stands for Cable News Network, but no one calls it that. CNN is known as CNN, and the domain name is CNN.com. Although this may be a simplistic explanation, your domain name should relate to your company name so your "brand" or company name easily can be recognized or memorized. For example, something like "www.wormstheword.com" relates to the company name and explains that the site will have something to do with worms.

Many professional Web designers recommend using keywords in your domain name rather than your company name. For example, the **www.strugglingteens.com** domain name specifically targets the industry of private schools and programs by using the keywords "struggling teens." Therefore, when you type the keywords "struggling teens" into the Google and Yahoo! search engines, this website pops up in the number one spot under the paid ads. Your domain name may have relevance in how some search engines rank your website, so embedding keywords into your domain name may help you achieve better search engine success. Another option you may consider is to purchase both domains names identifying your business and those using keywords. Put your website files on the domain name with the keywords and redirect the domain names with the company name to the keywords domain name. This will allow you to market the domain name with your company name, which helps with branding, and get the benefits of having the actual website located under a domain name with keywords. Some examples for a vermiculture business include **www.worms.com** or **www.vermicastings.com**.

Keywords built into website content and meta tags are essential to obtaining and maintaining visibility with these major search engines. Keywords are not something you implement once and forget; the keywords must be updated constantly to ensure immediate success in gaining visibility and to keep your site listed on the first page of the search engine results. Few people look beyond the first page of search engine results, so if you are located on page ten, or even page two, you may never be found.

Domain names should not be extremely long; this is going to be your URL address for your website, and the last thing you need is a long address no one can remember. Although some people may bookmark your page in their Internet browser, just as many, if not more, will not. You could lose valuable traffic if your website address is too long. If you are determined to have a long URL address, hyphenating the words will make it easier to read.

There was a time when domain names were readily available, but today you will find that many domain names already are registered by someone else. Typically, variations of your desired domain name are available, or perhaps other domain name extensions such as .org, .net, or .us. You can check the availability of a domain name by going to **www.godaddy.com**.

Search Engine Optimization Explained

While designing your website, you will read and hear a great deal about search engine optimization (SEO). **Search engine optimization (SEO)** is marketing vehicle used to increase a website's rank among search engines.

SEO involves developing your website in a way that will give you the maximum visibility with search engines. The more customers who see your products and information listed on Google, the greater the chance they will click on your business's link. Similarly, the closer your listing is to the top of the first page, the more clicks you will have. Understanding how SEO works is not difficult. Applying it to your site in a productive manner, however, takes considerable work. Website marketing has become very sophisticated due to increasing levels of available technology. With millions of websites competing for potential customers, it has become increasingly complex to ensure your site is found by interested buyers.

All Internet professionals have their own ideas on how to achieve high rankings. Search engines often are called spiders because they spread across the Internet looking for morsels of information to bring back to eat. In this case, it eats words and phrases, and it prefers the newest, most interesting food it can find. These spiders, or search engines, hunt, retrieve, and collect information based on the keywords requested by users. They are searching for the most relevant results. Search engine spiders, therefore, study the content of websites and rank content by hunting for specific phrases. They use two or more related words or phrases to garner the basic meaning of your page. Providing relevant, frequently updated copy with the right keywords and phrases will attract these spiders. Some keywords for a vermiculture business might include: worms, vermicompost, vermicastings, composting with worms, worm farming, and organic waste recycling worms.

Always keep in mind these two words: "fresh copy." Search engines seek new content. If your content grows outdated, or you rarely add new copy, the search engines will overlook your website. Your site's home page alone is not enough to keep the search engines happy. Blogs or extra pages with additional copy attached to your main website are required to rouse the interest of a search engine. Most important, you need to integrate the keywords, or those special words pertaining to your unique product or service, into your website design, copy, and videos. Use a different title and description with keywords on each page. Remember, the title of the page is the most important SEO factor. Also, do not forget to include a site map on your website. The search engine spiders cannot index pages if they are not available. Site maps help search engines understand the layout of your site. Using these keywords will help you "optimize" your website and be listed on one of the first two search engine pages. Most users will not go further than this to find the product or service they desire.

Overuse of SEO keywords and other banned tactics

Although using keywords on your site is necessary for SEO, overusing them can have a detrimental effect on your rankings. When websites are stuffed with keywords, so much so that the copy becomes unintelligible, search engines and customers know you are trying to scam the system. When this happens, the search engine spiders will stop visiting your site, and your site eventually will be ignored, resulting in low rankings.

The recommended keyword density ranges from 3 to 7 percent per article. Anything above this, even a 10 percent density, starts to look like keyword stuffing. It is even more important to have the correct density in the title, headings, and opening paragraphs. You can find keyword density tools online to help determine whether your keywords are within the correct range. A good free online keyword density tool can be found at **www.live-keyword-analysis.com**. You can also find synonyms for these keywords or rewrite the copy.

Hidden text, another forbidden SEO tactic, occurs when the text and links are designed in the same color as the background. Search engines not only will pass these over but also may punish you for such practices. This tactic is similar to hidden links or doorway pages, which are written into websites exclusively to achieve high rankings. Duplicate pages, with the same copy used repeatedly, are similarly nixed and no longer acceptable. The search engines are just as stringent on the number of links per page, monitoring the number of both outbound and inbound links. Programs also are used to measure your link density.

Another SEO turnoff is using small or unreadable type to fit more words into the design of the website. The biggest "no no" in terms of keywords is one that not only disturbs the search engines, but also your visitors as well. This involves adding keywords to the written text on your page that have nothing to do with the theme of the page. Keywords are important, but it is their use that matters.

Unfortunately, the SEO process is becoming increasingly complex because Google and the other search engines continually change their searching parameters. Because of this, many e-business owners use qualified SEO experts who are familiar with the latest changes. These professionals are hired to deliver SEO results by ensuring websites are readily seen by potential customers. Also, check with your site host, which may offer this service at an additional cost. Hiring a SEO expert can be costly, so you need to decide how much of your marketing budget will be spent on optimization. Consider taking on this responsibility yourself and put aside a couple of hours each day to ensure your website is getting the best placement. The more you are committed to the process, the better the results will be.

Some additional SEO tips

You can do some basic things to increase the chances that search engines will pick up your copy. These include the following:

- Commit yourself to SEO. It is something that you need to work on at least once a day. The more you are committed to the process, the better the results will be.

- Make SEO part of your marketing plan. You need clear SEO goals and an outline of how you expect to achieve them, at what cost.

- Be patient. After your website goes up, it will take at least two to three months of your hard editorial work to get the rankings you want in the search engines. The smaller and newer your business, the more difficult it becomes. That is why you want to work on this continually.

- Put at least a couple of topics of interest on your website every week using your keywords, which are original and not copied from someplace else. Search engines like new material. This also gives you an opportunity to write about any other information regarding your products.

- Build your website with a number of different pages and more copy. This gives you additional opportunities with the search engines. On each page you have online, there is another way to use keywords that will be searched and will reach specific potential customers. You can end up with hundreds of content pages, each one able to be indexed by search engines. Use the keywords that you find are most searched in your copy.

- Keep quality in mind at all times. You want strong editorial content that will be of interest to your readers and the search engines.

- Construct an interesting website, and always strive to make it better. That means adding content of interest to your main buyers.

- Do not forget your site map. Search engines cannot index pages that cannot be crawled. Your site map will help the search engines understand the layout of your pages.

- When you decide on your URL, think SEO. Keywords in your website name are quite useful.

- Make your copy interesting for your primary readers. They are the ones who will be coming to your site and buying your products and services.

- You want copy that is different from other websites. This is difficult for people in e-commerce. Put some time into your descriptions of products, and stay away from the boilerplates from the manufacturers. If you put your keywords into your descriptions, you will be ahead of the pack.

- Use keywords as anchor text when linking internally. These tell the search engines what the page is all about.

- Start a blog and participate with other related blogs.

Web Design Hardware Requirements

You do not need to invest significant funds to be able to create your own websites. You only need to have a reliable computer. Websites can be designed and tested on your personal or business computer, and you do not need to have your own Web server — in fact, you should avoid this cost. Many Web designers work exclusively from their laptop computers, which is a great way of having mobility, so you can keep working on your Web pages no matter where you are. A minimum recommendation for a laptop is an Intel® Core™2 Duo Processor,  although you do not need the fastest model on the market. In fact, any mid-range processor will more than meet your needs for a long time. On the desktop, the Intel Core 2 Quad models are highly suggested because of the ability to multitask effortlessly.

You also need to have a fast, reliable Internet connection. It really does not matter what you choose, as long as it is high-speed broadband that is reliable and cost-effective. Do not cut corners on your Internet speed, and do not use dial-up because it is far too slow, and you will become frustrated with its limitations quickly. You may want to use an external 1 GB hard drive for regular backups, while programs such as Carbonite™ are extremely useful for full backups of websites. You can get a free trial of Carbonite at **www.carbonite.com**.

For graphics editing, popular options include Corel® Paint Shop Pro® and Adobe Photoshop®. Some well-known examples of Web design software include Microsoft Office FrontPage, Microsoft Expression Web, and Adobe Dreamweaver. Other design applications such as Serif WebPlus offer great tools for the novice designer. That said, you do not need to invest significant funds into advanced Web design applications. There are also many freeware, or free software, offerings for both your Web design and graphic editing needs. Also, it is important to recognize that most Web hosting companies also provide easy-to-use website templates as part of your hosting package, which enables you to create a great looking site quickly and easily.

In the Web design and development communities, you will see two distinct groups: the Microsoft group and the Adobe group. The Adobe group uses Adobe Dreamweaver. Most Web developers consider Dreamweaver to be the professional Web designer's product of choice. In comparison, many used to consider Microsoft Office FrontPage to be the beginner's tool. Microsoft changed that with the release of Microsoft Expression Web, which matches up favorably with Dreamweaver. Microsoft no longer officially supports FrontPage, but it is still readily available for purchase. It is a good beginner tool that provides you with the environment where you create in design mode and the software writes the HTML code for you. WebPlus is also a great design application for those without any HTML experience.

Using Social Media and Networking

Social networking is the new "it" marketing vehicle. The main objective is to allow members who have the same interests to interact and exchange information. Many small businesses find social networking to be a great way to build and grow, especially in tough economic times when advertising budgets have been cut. Instead of paying for costly advertising, you are spreading information through word of mouth and websites that are free to use.

Although the exact definition is still being clarified, social networking essentially refers to an online community or group of users where people can connect and communicate with others. Although the actual format may vary from one network to another, communication takes place in many ways, such as blogs, email, instant messaging, forums, video, or chat rooms. Social networking connects people across the world in the privacy of their own homes, and the networking sites are usually free and instantaneous. People easily can stay in touch with current friends, seek old relationships, or establish new friendships. There are thousands of social networking sites, some that are primarily for social use and others that are for business networking.

How it will help

Members of social networking sites are numerous, which creates an excellent opportunity for an individual to expand and promote a business without having to pay for advertising. With social networking, you can build an image and develop your customer base. To increase their website traffic, many site owners quickly are realizing the value social networking sites have in drawing new customers. The following are some ideas on how to use social networking site to generate website traffic:

- Link from your website to your social network profile.

- Use social bookmarking to increase your website's exposure on social networking sites.

- Create and share videos and photos on Flickr® and YouTube® describing your business, products, and services.

- Use social networking forums to promote your business, website, and blog.

- Promote your business through your profile, with links to your home page.

Popular social networking sites

With the ever increasing number of people who use the Internet on a regular basis, these social websites have become a must, as this is the best and the easiest way for people to get connected with each other and stay in touch.

Orkut is a popular social networking site owned by Google. This social networking site has millions of users; 63 percent of Orkut traffic originates from Brazil, followed by India with 19.2 percent. Like other sites such as Facebook®, Orkut permits the creation of groups known as "communities" based on a designated subject and allows other people to join the communities. Orkut is an online community formed to liven up and stimulate your social life.

Facebook is the leading social networking site, with more than 800 million active users at the time of publication. Initially, Facebook was developed to connect university students, but over time, the site became available publicly, and its popularity exploded. The majority of users on Facebook are college and high school students, but this trend is shifting rapidly to people of all ages and backgrounds. On Facebook, it is extremely easy to add friends, send messages, and create communities or event invitations.

MySpace® is a social networking website that offers an interactive platform for all its users. It allows the sharing of files, pictures, and even music videos. You can view the profiles of your friends, relatives, and any other users; you also can create and share blogs with each other. Users often compare Facebook to MySpace, but there is a differing amount of personalization allowed when designing pages on the two sites. While MySpace enables users to create customized profiles using HTML and CSS, Facebook only gives the option of placing simple text on a profile. The most prominent feature that makes MySpace unique among other sites is its affiliate program. An affiliate program is a form of Web advertising that rewards the affiliates, or those doing the marketing on their site for another company, for driving traffic to the advertiser or for subsequent transactions. If the affiliate product you are selling has a broad appeal, you may want to consider using MySpace to market your product, as you will be able to reach a large crowd quickly.

YouTube is another social networking site owned by Google. YouTube is the largest video sharing network site in the world, and it is a great place to do video marketing. To become a member of YouTube, go to the "Signup" page, choose a username and password, enter your information, and click the "Signup" button.

Digg™ is a place to unearth and share content retrieved anywhere throughout the Web. Digg allows you to directly network with people and directly sell products. Once a post is submitted, it appears on a list in the selected category. From there, it will either fall in ranking or rise in raking, depending on how people vote. Digg is actually what is known as a "social bookmarking" site. Social bookmarking is a method where users can share, organize, and search bookmarks of Web pages or articles in an online, public forum instead of on their browsers; many social bookmarking sites allow users to vote on or recommend bookmarks, which allows content to grow more popular and be seen by a wider range of people the higher it is ranked. You submit your content to Digg, and other Digg users — known as Diggers — will review and rate it. Once it is rated high enough, your content may get posted on the home page of Digg, which gets thousands of visitors a day, potentially driving tons of traffic to your website or blog.

Twitter™ is different from other social networking sites, and the popularity of Twitter has grown at an amazing rate. Twitter is actually a form of microblogging, which is a Web service that allows users to broadcast short messages — in Twitter's case 140 characters or fewer — to other users. With Twitter, you can let your friends know what you are doing throughout the day right from your phone or computer. When you sign up with Twitter, you can post and receive messages (known as a "tweet") with your Twitter account, and the site sends your tweet out to your friends and subscribers. In turn, you receive all the messages sent from those you wish to follow, including friends, family, and even celebrities. In essence, Twitter is a cell phone texting-based social network.

Flickr is a photo and video sharing website that lets you organize and store your photos online. You can upload from your desktop, send by email, or use your camera phone. It has features to eliminate red eye, crop a photo, or use your creative side with fonts and effects. Google Picasa® is another great photo sharing and storing application.

Popular business networking sites

The following sites offer businesses opportunities to network with other business owners.

Biznik® (www.biznik.com): The tagline for this site is: "Business networking that doesn't suck." It is geared directly to entrepreneurs and business owners, with a number of different communities.

Ecademy (www.ecademy.com): This site provides extra tools to build your business, such as networking events, webinars on online topics, and the ability to locate members with specific knowledge.

Fast Pitch (www.fastpitchnetworking.com): Fast Pitch reports it is growing faster than any other social network for professionals. It allows you to set up your own profile page and network with other businesspeople.

Konnects® (www.konnects.com): This site gives each member a profile page and allows you to join communities, meet other members, and network with professionals with similar interests.

LinkedIn® (www.linkedin.com): This site allows you to connect and network with others in your field that can use your abilities and/or services.

StartupNation® (www.startupnation.com): This site provides active forums with a wide variety of subjects for businesses.

StumbleUpon (www.stumbleupon.com): This site allows you to post any information of value and interest to others.

Upspring™ (www.upspring.com): This site gives you the opportunity to increase exposure and attract more customers. You can sign up free and get a profile page, find and join groups, and increase your networking activities.

Xing (www.xing.com): Xing is an active group of professionals looking for ways to network with people of interest.

In establishing a business, it is important to plan for marketing and publicity in a format that will draw customers to you. A website will allow customers, near and far, to find you. Most people, when looking for a specific business, will do a Web search and positioning your business with a well-designed and visible website will give you a worm up on the competition.

Conclusion

"To revolt is a natural tendency of life. Even a worm turns against the foot that crushes it. In general, the vitality and relative dignity of an animal can be measured by the intensity of its instinct to revolt."

MIKHAIL BAKUNIN

Creating a worm farm, whether on a small, medium, or large scale can be a rewarding learning experience at any age and is a great family project that could even turn into a profitable business venture. The process of composting with worms has been practiced throughout history and is a great method of recycling organic waste, while creating a beneficial organic gardening by-product.

Worms long have been considered the gardener's best friend and one of the hardest working creatures in a well-tended and productive garden. Generally misunderstood as "yucky," the worm often has gotten a bad reputation beyond the walls of the gardening world. This book has provided information on their importance in recycling, gardening, and as an educational tool. Not to mention, how the meager earthworm can turn into a profitable business idea.

Earthworms in nature play a vital role in the recycling process of being able to turn dead materials back into living organisms. Sadly, because of their bad reputation, they often are overlooked in their important and vital role. By using the worm's strength as a hard worker, you will see how they can turn tons of waste into something of value for your garden. As a result, your vegetables, houseplants, perennials, and lawn will become healthier and more productive.

Miscellaneous Worms

Alternate Worm Bin

If you live in a warmer climate, you have the luxury of being able to set up your vermicomposting system outdoors. Cinderblocks make an excellent barrier to create a vermicomposting system, and they will not mold or become airtight like wood or plastic. However, you still will have to monitor all conditions, such as temperature and moisture levels, in your outside worm bins if you want to keep your worms in full, garbage-chomping health.

1. Decide where in your yard to build the outdoor worm bin. Find a spot that is out of direct sunlight.

2. Stack cinderblocks on three sides of a square or rectangle shape, about four feet tall.

3. Add cinderblocks to the fourth side about a foot tall, this will allow you easier access to the bin.

4. Add bedding, worms, and organic material.

What to Feed/Not Feed your Worms

Worm menu:

- Fruits
- Fruit peels
- Vegetables
- Vegetable peels and tops
- Coffee grounds and filters
- Newspaper (black ink only)
- Tea leaves
- Tea bags
- Kelp
- Pasta
- Rice
- Melons
- Peels
- Flowers and stems
- Grass clippings
- Leaves (brown and green)
- Eggshells
- Cereal
- Cake
- Muffins
- Pizza crusts
- Composted manure from horses, rabbits, sheep, chickens, cows, or goats

What not to feed your worms: Foods such as eggs, meats, and dairy products are enjoyed by worms but are not recommended for home vermicomposting systems, as they can smell and attract unwanted animals and pests to your bin. It also has been discovered that citrus products in excess can kill off worm populations in your bin. The following list is contains some good guidelines of foods to avoid feeding your worms:

- Non-biodegradable items: Items such as plastic bags, rubber bands, aluminum foil, glass, and sponges are not biodegradable, and the worms cannot process them.

- Dog and cat feces: Disease organisms present in cat and dog feces are harmful to humans. Toxoplasma gondii, for example, is found in cat feces and can be transmitted through a mother to her unborn baby and cause brain damage.

- Meat waste and bones: Decaying meat should not be used in a home bin, as it can produce offensive odors and attract unwanted organisms and animals to the worm bin.

- Heavily spiced foods

- Hair

- Dairy products: Milk, yogurt, butter, and eggs should not be included in the worm bin.

- Poisonous plants

- Oils

- Soaps

- Salt

- Wood ashes

Worm Tracking

Monthly Sample Worm Tracker

The worm bin should be monitored on a regular basis to ensure proper aeration, temperature, correct amount of grit provided for proper digestion, pH level, new bedding, and proper feeding. The following chart will help you keep track of all of theses variables to ensure the health of your worms. You can copy this chart on a copier or make a copy in your notebook.

Month: _____

	Week 1	Week 2	Week 3	Week 4
Temperature				
pH Level				
Bedding type				
Bedding changed				
Food added				
Grit added				
Food disappearing?				
Worms getting larger?				
Unwanted bugs				
Baby worms				
Eggs or cocoons				
Notes:				

Worm checklist

1. ***Odor level:*** If the worms in your vermicomposting system begin to smell, it is an indication of a larger problem that needs to be looked into. The bin should not have a foul smell.

2. ***Eating habits:*** There might be a problem if you notice that your worms have changed their eating habits. Are they eating less than they used to? Are they consuming more? If there is a noticeable difference in the worms' eating habits, check the conditions in the bin to ensure they meet your breed's requirements.

3. ***Light them up:*** Worms, when exposed to light, should quickly try to bury themselves. If they do not do this, they might be sick. Open the bin and shine a flashlight in. If the worms move quickly to hide, they are healthy. If they do not move or seem sluggish, something could be wrong. Double-check all the conditions in the bin to ensure proper requirements.

4. ***Know your worms:*** Any good pet owner or farmer will tell you it is important to get to know your worms and their regular habits. By observing the worms when they are healthy, worm owners will be able to pick out unhealthy worms when they fall sick.

5. ***Check their slime level:*** Every worm has slime, or thin mucus, on its body. If the worms seem dry, this could be a sign of a larger problem. If the worms seem too dry, check all the conditions in the bin to make sure there are proper moisture, aeration, temperature, and pH levels.

Just for Fun: Worm Charming

The art of worm calling is referred to as worm charming, worm grunting, and worm fiddling. It is based on the technique that certain animals like turtles, gulls, and kiwis use to call worms to the surface for food. The process involves sending vibrations down into the soil that worms respond to, causing them to come to the surface. Worm charming runs the gamut from hobbyist to professional and competitive. Professional worm charmers call worms to the surface and collect them for farming and resale purposes. Worm calling competitions are worldwide and even include annual festivals along with the competitions.

One of the largest annual worm calling festivals is in Sopchoppy, Florida. The Sopchoppy Worm Gruntin' Festival (**www.wormgruntinfestival.com**) takes place yearly in April. It includes competitions, vendors, live music, games, and the crowning of a Worm Grunter's King, Queen, and Princess.

There are a variety of theories as to why worms respond to vibrations in the soil. Some point to a natural instinct to avoid predators such as moles, whose digging makes vibrations in the soil. To escape the underground predator, worms come to the surface. Another theory points to the idea that vibrations are similar to the rhythm of pounding rain. Worms often come to the surface in a rainstorm to avoid drowning or to mate.

Regardless, you can experiment and amaze your friends by perfecting your worm charming techniques. This also makes a fun experiment for kids.

For this technique, you will need two wooden sticks, one smooth and the other notched. Both should be about three to four feet in length. Take the smooth stick and pound it into the ground about 6 to 18 inches: the further down, the more optimal your chance of getting worms will be. Take the notched stick and rub it against the smooth stick in a sawing motion. It will take a few minutes for the worms to begin to surface.

Sample Business Plan

Getting Wiggly with It
Business Plan

5 Worm Hollow
Early Bird, KY

Melissa Maven
president

December 5, 2011

Table of Contents

Mission Statement

At *Getting Wiggly with It*, we value the importance of recycling and reducing organic waste, while informing our customers about the unique benefits of vermicomposting. We pride ourselves on selling the highest quality worms for home and large-scale vermicomposting purposes.

Executive Summary

Getting Wiggly with It is a vermiculture business that will be located at 5 Worm Hole Hollow in Early Bird, Kentucky. The location is in a large barn next to Robin's Daycare that will house the worm farm as well as executive offices and a storefront in the future. *Getting Wiggly with It* is a vermiculture business that raises and sells worms for vermicomposting purposes, while educating our customers about the importance and value of recycling organic waste.

Company Description

Getting Wiggly with It is a vermiculture business that will farm, sell, and educate its customers about vermicomposting on a small and large-scale basis. The company plans to sell the following items: red wiggler worms, ready-made vermicomposting systems, bedding, worm tea, vermicastings, and other related supplies. In addition to selling, the company also will provide workshops and classes on vermicomposting, recycling, and using organic fertilizers in the garden. We also plan to reach out to the community and help local schools, senior centers, food banks, etc. that will benefit from having their own vermicomposting system to recycle organic waste.

Once we have established our farm, the company plans to branch out to the Internet, where we will sell worms and other supplies via the Web. Once the business is established, we also plan to develop a variety of books on vermicomposting and worm farming as a valuable resource for information on farming worms and creating vermicompost.

Currently, there are not any vermiculture businesses in Early Bird, Kentucky, or any of the surrounding towns.

Organization and Management

During the first year in business, Melissa Maven will act as the owner and president. Ophelia Grimes will join the team once the startup loan from the bank comes through as vice president and chief worm farmer.

We plan to outsource the accounting and bookkeeping needs of the business to a third-party. As the business grows and prospers, the company may hire an administrative assistant and an accountant or bookkeeper to be a part of the full-time staff. For now, there will be two employees of the business: Melissa Maven and Ophelia Grimes, who will both take on a variety of roles within the business. In the future, additional worm farmers, salespeople, and educators as well as a marketing and public relations person will be hired to join the team.

To start, the business will operate out of large barn that sits on the property of Melissa Maven's home residence. This means that the business will have its own designated building to house supplies and set up the vermicomposting bins that house the worms.

In the area where the home and barn is located, the county allows home-based business owners to sell from their property as long as they are registered with the town and pay appropriate taxes. Because the barn is large enough to allow for the business to add staff in the next one to two years, the plan is to keep the business running out of the barn and eventually add formal office space to the existing building. Pending the success of the business, the company also plans to add a storefront to the bottom level of the two-story barn with the administrative offices being moved to the second floor and the worm farms to a larger location within the barn.

Market Analysis

Industry background

The worm farming industry is currently operating in a market where the need for experienced professionals is growing. For one, people are turning to growing more of their own food at home and are looking for an alternative to commercial fertilizers to support their home-based gardens. Schools, food banks, group homes, and other service-related industries are looking for ways to cut down on waste and are turning to vermicomposting as an effective and easy method to recycle that waste.

Target markets

Getting Wiggly with It will target the home hobby gardener, small and medium-scale farmers, churches, schools, group homes, small hospitals, and other service-related industries looking for organic gardening fertilizers or organic waste recycling units.

Product Description

The company is a vermiculture business that will farm, sell, and educate customers in Early Bird, Kentucky, and the surrounding towns about worms and their use in composting organic waste.

Marketing and Promotions

The company will distribute fliers/brochures to local schools, farms, small-scale businesses and service industries in the area. Melissa and Ophelia also will hold free seminars/classes at the local library to educate people about the use of worms in composting and will provide information on their business at the free classes. They plan to promote the business through the local farmers markets with a booth for the company to sell their worms and supplies and provide information on vermicomposting. They also plan to advertise on the free listing boards on the Internet, as well as around town. In addition, they will start an email and Facebook campaign to get the word out about the business.

Operations

Getting Wiggly with It possesses a unique position in the market because of the unique expertise of Melissa Maven, the owner and president of the business. Melissa has worked with worms for the past ten years as a manager for a large-scale gardening company. She also has taught at the university level on topics such as recycling, vermicomposting, gardening, and substantial farming.

Ophelia Grimes has worked alongside Melissa for the past three years as a worm farmer at the gardening company. Before that, Ophelia set up and maintained a large-scale worm farm at the University of Vermont in its recycling department. The two women have more than 20 years experience in the field.

Strengths

Getting Wiggly with It will be the only business of its kind in the local area. Experts in the field with more 20 years of experience will run the business. The women starting up the business also have qualified for a government business startup grant of $2,000.

Weaknesses

Although the company has the expertise and the location to start up, it does not have the finances and will need to pursue a business loan to help with startup costs in addition to the government grant.

Financials

Startup Requirements

STARTUP EXPENSES

Legal	$50
Stationery, etc.	$50
Brochures	$82
Insurance	$150
Worm farm equipment	$4,000
Total startup expenses	**$4,332**

STARTUP ASSETS

Cash required	$22,500
Other current assets	$0
Long-term assets	$0
Total assets	**$22,500**
Total requirements	**$26,832**

Startup Funding

Startup expenses to fund	$4,332
Startup assets to fund	$22,500
Total funding required	**$26,832**

ASSETS

Non-cash assets from startup	$0
Cash requirements from startup	$22,500
Additional cash raised	$0
Cash balance on starting date	$22,500
Total assets	**$22,500**

LIABILITIES AND CAPITAL	
Liabilities	
Current borrowing	$1,500
Long-term liabilities	$22,500
Accounts payable (outstanding bills)	$100
Other current liabilities (interest-free)	$0
Total liabilities	**$24,100**
Capital	
Planned investment	
Owner	$3,800
Other	$0
Additional investment requirement	$0
Total planned investment	**$4,000**
Loss at startup (startup expenses)	($4,332)
Total capital	**($332)**
Total capital and liabilities	**$22,500**
Total funding	**$26,832**

Sales Forecast

SALES	YEAR 1	YEAR 2	YEAR 3
Product and services	$47,500	$95,000	$190,000
Other	$0	$0	$0
Total sales	**$47,500**	**$95,000**	**$190,000**
DIRECT COST OF SALES	YEAR 1	YEAR 2	YEAR 3
Fees	$0	$0	$0
Other	$0	$0	$0
Subtotal direct cost of sales	**$0**	**$0**	**$0**

Pro Forma Profit and Loss

	YEAR 1	YEAR 2	YEAR 3
Sales	**$47,500**	**$95,000**	**$190,000**
Direct cost of sales	$0	$0	$0
Payroll	$27,500	$55,000	$110,000
Other	$0	$0	$0
Total cost of sales	**$27,500**	**$55,000**	**$110,000**
Gross margin	$20,000	$40,000	$80,000
Gross margin %	42.00%	42.00%	42.00%

Operating Expenses

SALES AND MARKETING EXPENSES			
Sales and marketing payroll	$0	$0	$0
Advertising/promotion	$1,000	$1,250	$1,500
Bank service charges	$510	$500	$750
Contributions	$125	$150	$150
Dues & subscriptions	$500	$625	$750
Total sales and marketing expenses	**$2,135**	**$2,525**	**$3,150**
Sales and marketing %	4.49%	2.66%	1.66%
GENERAL AND ADMINISTRATIVE EXPENSES			
Marketing/promotion	$3,250	$3,000	$6,250
Depreciation	$0	$0	$0
Telephone/cell phone/Internet	$1,860	$2,040	$2,500
Recruitment	$750	$790	$1,000

Referral fees	$100	$125	$250
Office supplies	$1,000	$1,500	$2,000
Postage	$530	$625	$750
Printing	$1,750	$2,000	$2,500
Professional fees	$3,500	$2,500	$3,750
Payroll taxes	$0	$0	$0
Maintenance and repairs	$160	$375	$1,000
Total general and administrative expenses	**$12,900**	**$12,955**	**$20,000**
General and administrative %	27.17%	13.63%	10.53%
OTHER EXPENSES:			
Other payroll	$0	$0	$0
Consultants	$0	$0	$0
Miscellaneous	$525	$250	$500
Total other expenses	**$525**	**$250**	**$500**
Other %	1.10%	0.26%	0.26%
Total operating expenses	**$15,560**	**$15,730**	**$43,650**
Net profit	**$4,435**	**$22,920**	**$56,350**
Net profit/sales	**9.34%**	**24.13%**	**29.66%**

Conclusion

Getting Wiggly with It is expected to be profitable within the first two to three years in business. The primary basis of this success is the knowledge, experience, and contacts that the owner has and will continue to build while owning the business.

As the company continues to grow, the owner intends on adding employees as needed. Her barn/office will hold up to ten employees, including Melissa.

Supporting Documentation

The following documentation for *Getting Wiggly with It* is included:

- Copies of *Getting Wiggly with It* principals' résumés
- Tax returns and personal financial statements of *Getting Wiggly with It* principals for the last three years
- A copy of *Getting Wiggly with It* licenses and certifications
- A copy of *Getting Wiggly with It* purchase agreement
- Copies of letters of intent from *Getting Wiggly with It* suppliers

APPENDIX C

Resources

Publications

Earthworm Digest
P.O. Box 544
Eugene, OR 97440-0544
www.wormdigest.org
A quarterly newsletter all about worms

Websites

CalRecycle, California: **www.calrecycle.ca.gov/Organics/Worms/WormFact.htm**

City Farmer, Canada's office of Urban Agriculture: **http://cityfarmer.org/wormcomp61.html**

Cornell University: **http://compost.css.cornell.edu/worms/basics.html**

Environmental Education for Kids (EEK), Wisconsin: **http://dnr.wi.gov/ org/caer/ce/eek/earth/recycle/compost2.htm**

Massachusetts Department of Environmental Protection: **www.mass.gov/ dep/recycle/reduce/vermi.htm**

Red Worm Composting: **www.redwormcomposting.com**

University of Nebraska-Lincoln: **http://lancaster.unl.edu/pest/ resources/vermicompost107.shtml**

University of Vermont: **www.uvm.edu/~recycle/?Page=compost/vermic omposting.html&SM=compost/compost-menu.html**

U.S. Environmental Protection Agency: **www.epa.gov/wastes/conserve/ rrr/composting/vermi.htm**

Washington State University: **http://whatcom.wsu.edu/ag/compost/ Redwormsedit.htm**

Shopping Guide

Acme Worm Farm
4731 N. Edgebrooke Place
Tucson, AZ 85705
520-750-8056

www.acmewormfarm.com
Worms and vermicomposting supplies

Gaiam®
877-989-6321
www.gaiam.com
Natural organic items including worm bins

Organic Worm Composting
Hoykim Industries
3295 Man-Cal Rd
Reedsville, WI 54230
920-716-1971
www.organicwormcomposting.com
Organic gardening and worm supplies

Planet Natural (retail)
1251 N. Rouse Ave.
Bozeman, MT 59715
www.planetnatural.com
General gardening items, natural garden supplies, and
vermicomposting supplies

Uncle Jim's Worm Farm
800-873-0555
www.unclejimswormfarm.com
Worms, books, and supplies

Glossary

acidic: Having the characteristics of acids; tests lower than 7 on a pH meter.

aerate: To supply with or expose to air.

aerobic: Anything that requires and feeds off oxygen to live.

alimentary canal: A tube that runs the length of the worm's body from mouth to anus. The food passes through the tube and is broken down through the varying tubal sections. The sections of the alimentary canal include the buccal cavity (a mouth without teeth or jaws), the pharynx (suction pump for food), the esophagus, the crop (stores food), the gizzard (grinds food), and the intestine (digestion and nutrient absorption).

alkaline: Testing higher than a 7 on the pH scale.

anaerobic bacteria: Bacteria that grow in environments that lack oxygen and can create an acidic product that is harmful to your worms.

anterior: Toward the front part of the worm.

antinomycetes: Rod-shaped members of the bacteria family.

bacteria: Microorganisms that are generally one-celled and can exist either independently or be dependent on another organism for life.

bed-run: A mixture of worms at all stages of life from cocoon to sexual maturity.

bedding: Organic materials used in worm composting systems.

biomass: The weight of the worms.

breeders: Worms that have reached sexual maturity and can reproduce.

brown material waste: Non-living organic waste that includes dried leaves, newsprint, dead plants, brown paper bags, dry grass clippings, and straw.

carbon dioxide emissions: a colorless, odorless gas that is formed by the combustion of carbons. It is non-poisonous and is in the respiration of all living organisms.

castings: The excrement of worms.

chemical decomposers: Microscopic organisms such as bacteria, fungi, protozoa, and antinomycetes.

clitellum: Appears as a band or saddle around the worm, its location varies by species, and it indicates that the worm is sexually mature and old enough to breed. The clitellum can appear as a swollen area and is often a different color than the rest of the worm.

cocoon: An egg case. Worm cocoons contain from two to 20 worms each.

commercial fertilizer: A fertilizer that is manufactured chemically. It is not a naturally derived fertilizer like manure or vermicastings.

compostable materials: Organic materials that will break down in a compost bin.

composting: A natural process by which organic waste is biologically reduced into humus.

consumers: Organisms that gather energy by eating other organisms or food particles.

decomposers: Organisms that break down organic matter in the dead bodies of other plants or animals.

decomposition: The breaking down of organic matter into basic components and elements.

deep-burrowers: Worms that build deep burrows, or tunnels, down deep in the soil, sometimes to six feet. These worms take food, drag it down into their burrows, and provide a lot of oxygen to the soil in the process. Deep burrowers do not hibernate but do retreat to the bottoms of their burrows during the colder months.

diatomaceous earth: A light-colored porous rock composed of the shells of diatoms.

earthworm: A segmented terrestrial worm.

feedstock: The organic materials fed to worms that include the bedding material as well as the organic waste.

fertilizer: A substance that is added to the soil to supply plant nutrients.

first-consumers: Physical decomposers in a vermicomposting system, such as beetles and worms, that do the majority of the initial breakdown of organic waste into smaller particles.

fungi: Parasites that feed on dead organic material and reproduce by means of spores.

green material waste: Organic materials to feed the worms, or other compost piles, that include vegetable peelings, rotting fruit, leaves (not dried), plant trimmings, spent flowers, coffee grounds, tea leaves, and eggshells.

gizzard: An organ found in the digestive tract of some animals, like worms, that serves as a stomach to grind up foods.

grit: An additive like fine soil, eggshells, rock dust, and coffee grinds that aids a worm's gizzard in digesting and grinding up foods into smaller pieces.

habitat: A place where an organism lives.

hermaphroditic: An organism that possesses both female and male organs.

humus: A dark blackish-brown material of partially or fully decayed organic matter.

in-vessel composting: A method by which organic waste is placed into contained equipment such as a silo, drum, or concrete-lined trench.

leachate: The name of the liquid released during the composting process. Leachate can contain harmful bacteria and other substances that are leached from the compost into a liquid form.

litter-dwellers: Worms that live on the topmost layer, or litter layer, of the soil. These guys usually are found under fallen leaves or needles on the forest floor.

mesophilic: An organism that grows at moderate temperature.

microbes: A microscopic organism, such as a bacterium.

microorganisms: Tiny organisms that cannot be seen, that are present in the soil.

oligochaetelogy: The study of earthworms.

on-site composting: Backyard composting, or composting on the premises.

organic matter: Plant and animal residues such as leaves, trimmings, and manure in various stages of decomposition.

pH level: A measurement of potential hydrogen, or levels of acidity to alkalinity on a scale.

pH scale: A number scale that ranges from one to 14. The lower numbers on the scale, the more acid the soil is. The higher the number is on the scale, the more alkaline the soil is said to be. The number 7, in the middle of the scale, is said to be a neutral pH.

pest: An organism that is annoying to humans or other organisms.

photophobic: An organism that shuns both artificial and natural light.

physical decomposers: Not-so-microscopic organisms, such as worms, snails, beetles, centipedes, and even mites, that aid in the decomposition process.

polyaromatic hydrocarbons (PAH): Environmental pollutants that can be found in coal, oil, and tar. PAHs are a by-product produced when these items are burned as fuel. As a pollutant, some of the compounds released have been identified as harmful carcinogens and other cell-damaging components.

protozoa: Single-celled organisms that can be divided only with the help of a host.

recycle: To use something over again.

search engine optimization (SEO): The process of improving the visibility of a website or a Web page in search engines without paying someone to promote it.

second-consumers: The bacteria, fungi, protozoa and antinomycetes that step in after the first-consumers to initiate the composting process and begin to create heat. These microorganisms are considered mesophilic and work best at temperatures between 10 and 45 degrees C (50 and 113 degrees F).

setae: The name for the bristles on a worm's body. The setae's main function is movement, and they vary in length and shape by worm variety. The earthworm extends it body to move, anchors itself via the setae, and then contracts its body. This process is referred to as a step.

shallow-dwellers: Worms that live on the top 12 inches or so of the soil and burrow randomly throughout the soil without making permanent burrows. During the cold seasons, these worms burrow deeper and hibernate to avoid being frozen.

soil: A mixture of organic material in which plants grow.

static pile composting: Composting in one large pile. In order to aerate the pile properly, layers of loose agents such as shredded newspaper or wood chips are layered in between organic waste, similar to creating "bedding" in a vermicomposting pile. These piles sometimes are placed over a network of pipes that add air in or draw air out of the pile.

thermophiles: An organism that requires high temperatures for normal growth and development.

third-consumers: After the first-consumers and the second-consumers, the temperature within the compost pile increases and the next level of microorganisms step in, called the third-consumers. Referred to as thermophiles, these guys operate best at temperatures between 45 and 75 degrees C (113 and 167 degrees F).

top dressing: A material used as an additive to the top layers of soil.

transplanting: Moving a plant from one location to another.

vermicastings: Or worm castings, are the by-product, or manure, of worms that make a fabulous fertilizer.

vermicomposting: The process of using worms to decompose organic waste and turn it into a natural fertilizer.

vermicomposting system: The term used for the worm bin and vermicomposting process.

vermiculture: The controlled method of worm farming or raising earthworms.

volatile organic compounds (VOC): A man-made or naturally occurring chemical compound that evaporates into the air at a low temperature. VOCs contribute to air pollution but are not considered acutely toxic due to their low concentration level. VOCs can, however, affect both the environment and human health. Due to their low level of concentration, symptoms caused by exposure to VOCs are slow to develop and are compounded over time.

windrow method composting: Turned composting also is referred to as the windrow method. Organic waste is collected and formed into long piles, or rows. These rows are ideally 4 to 8 feet in height and between 14 and 16 feet wide. These piles are called "windrows," and their size allows for a pile large enough to generate heat and maintain temperatures while being small enough to allow oxygen flow to their core. The piles require aeration, which is done by periodically turning the piles either manually or mechanically.

worm bedding: The organic material used for the worms to "nest in" and start eating.

worm bin: The container that has been properly prepared for the worms to live in while they consume organic waste.

worm tea: Water in which finished worm compost, or vermicasts, has been steeped to create a nutrient-rich "tea" for plants.

Bibliography

Appelhof, Mary. *Worms Eat My Garbage.* Flowerfield Enterprises, LLC., 1997.

The A-Z Guide to Federal Employment Laws For the Small Business Owner. Atlantic Publishing Group, Inc., 2010.

Brown, Bruce C. *How to Build Your Own Web Site With Little or No Money: The Complete Guide for Business and Personal Use.* Atlantic Publishing Group, Inc., 2009.

Fontana, PK. *Choosing the Right Legal Form of Business: The Complete Guide to Becoming a Sole Proprietor, Partnership, LLC, or Corporation.* Atlantic Publishing Group, Inc., 2010.

Martin, Deborah L., and Grace Gershuny, editors. *The Rodale Book of Composting.* Rodale Press, 1992.

Nancarrow, Loren, and Janet Hogan Taylor. *The Worm Book*. Ten Speed Press, 1998.

Wasnak, Lynn. *How to Open & Operate a Financially Successful Landscaping, Nursery, or Lawn Service Business: With Companion CD-ROM*. Atlantic Publishing Group, Inc., 2009.

Wilkinson, Tom. *Beyond Compost*. Tom Wilkinson, 1999.

Author Bio

Wendy M. Vincent is a writer who has worked on a variety of writing projects from corporate communication materials to magazine articles to books and everything in-between. Her past book projects include *The Complete Guide to Growing Healing and Medicinal Herbs* (Atlantic Publishing, 2011) and a travel guide to Mystic, Connecticut (Channel Lake, 2012). She is also an editor for an online news publication. For additional information on her work, visit **www.wendymvincent.com.**

Descended from generations of farmers and home gardeners, Vincent has a yard abundant in perennial, vegetable, and herb gardens. In addition to a healthy garden full of worms, she also keeps a four-tiered, home vermicomposting system in her basement, where she recycles organic kitchen and yard waste as food for her worms and uses the vermicompost in her gardens.

Index